Betsy,

Once you choose hope

anything :

xx,
Jenn Grace

House on Fire

House on Fire

Finding Resilience, Hope, and Purpose in the Ashes

Jenn T. Grace

PUBLISH
YOUR
PURPOSE
PRESS

For permission requests, write to the publisher, addressed "Attention: Permissions Coordinator," at the address below.

Publish Your Purpose Press
141 Weston Street, #155
Hartford, CT, 06141

The opinions expressed by the Author are not necessarily those held by Publish Your Purpose Press.

Ordering Information: Quantity sales and special discounts are available on quantity purchases by corporations, associations, and others. For details, contact the publisher at the address above.

Manuscript Strategist: Fern Pessin
Edited by: Heather B. Habelka, Karen Ang, and Nan Price
Cover design by: Tri Widyatmaka
Foredge design by: Masha Shubin
Headshot by: Mike Marques
Typeset by: Medlar Publishing Solutions Pvt Ltd., India

Printed in the United States of America.
ISBN: 978-1-951591-09-0 (hardcover)
ISBN: 978-1-951591-13-7 (paperback)
ISBN: 978-1-951591-14-4 (ebook)

Library of Congress Control Number: 2020909652

First edition, June 2020.

The mission of Publish Your Purpose Press is to discover and publish authors who are striving to make a difference in the world. We give marginalized voices power and a stage to share their stories, speak their truth, and impact their communities. Do you have a book idea you would like us to consider publishing? Please visit PublishYourPurposePress.com for more information.

Dedication

This book is dedicated to:

My parents. I now understand they were both doing the best that they could in the circumstances they were given.

All families who are struggling with mental health issues that consume your lives. Don't give up and don't be afraid to speak up. The world needs to hear your unique and invisible stories.

To those who are feeling alone, abandoned, orphaned, or isolated. My wish is that this will show you a path forward and give you a glimpse of hope in an otherwise dark time.

Table of Contents

A Letter from the Author

Dear Reader,

While writing this memoir, I have attempted to relay all the events portrayed to the best of my memory. It has been cobbled together with assistance from journals, photos, and "remember when …" family tales told over holiday dinners and special occasions.

Obviously, it is written from my own perspective, which quite likely is different from how others in and out of my life would re-tell the same stories. Certain incidents are more vivid, yet entire blocks of time are missing. And, for many of us, we may often have only one small snippet of a memory from a particular year of our past. That's because of a dear friend I've come to know so well: Dissociation.

Like many people, I recollect and share my stories as vignettes. My life— like yours, I'm sure—involved coping strategies, arguments, laughter, challenges, and many, many obstacles. The details of my story are likely different than yours, but the fact that we struggle is universal.

I have changed the names of people, towns, locations, and other identifying details to offer as much respect, anonymity, and privacy as I could to those involved, while still being able to share my story authentically.

It has taken a great deal of courage for me to come to a place of healing and forgiveness in my life so that I can share my story with the world. It is not without deep fears of exposing myself in very vulnerable ways. My life has been one of trauma, loss, obstacles, and triumph, and I did my best to remain as fair to everyone I included in this book. What we know to be true is that bad things happen to good people and good people make bad decisions. It is what we do after those decisions that matters.

There will be people who may not feel good about how they are written about and to them I would like to share a quote by Anne Lamott:

> *You own everything that happened to you. Tell your stories. If people wanted you to write warmly about them, they should have behaved better.*

I invite you to join this ride with me, learn, laugh, cope, and come out on the other side a little better than when you started this book.

With love, gratitude, and deep empathy for what you are going through,

Jenn T Grace

Wreckage from the Fire

Age 18

Going through black muck and household rubble after everything was over and the embers had cooled in the morning, I could see that almost everything I owned was gone. Head down, hugging my coat to my body on a gray, cold, late fall day, I shuffled through the ashes, kicking away clumps of mystery items, on the hunt for some remnant of my 18 years of life that would bring me joy. My eyes misted as I found every hard-earned softball and sports trophy melted beyond recognition. My lucky softball glove that helped me win all of those trophies, gone. All my clothes, every championship-winning sports jacket of mine in the hallway closet, gone. My entire bedroom—all soggy from fire hose spray and permanently smoke-darkened—gone forever.

My cat Pumpkin died while our three other cats miraculously survived. It felt like every single place in the house where *my* items were was burnt to ashes. Our house was destroyed; the frame of our family ruined—charred beyond recognition.

My sister, Amanda, and my mother had been in the house when the fire started. My mom's official story was that Amanda was playing alone in the family room, tried to light a candle, and "accidentally" set the recliner on fire, which then caught the bookcase behind it on fire, and, subsequently, the rest of that room, and then the house. I directed my fury over the loss of my things and dreams for the future at my sister for the destruction she had caused.

Tears rolled silently down my cheeks as I uncovered my tattered, melted, and singed E.T. doll. From a very early age, I had declared that E.T. would be my wedding bouquet. That hope remained until I was 18 and standing in those ashes. Now that vision of my future wedding was also destroyed. A smoldering ember remained in my soul as I carried E.T.'s charred remains out of the gutted house. It was as if his plastic and fabric stuffed body—wrapped in a towel—was equal to that of my deceased cat.

As I got in my red Jeep Wrangler—the car I inherited when my father passed away a few years prior—to leave the wreckage, I took comfort knowing that only two weeks before, I happened to have cleared out my bedroom. Many important treasures, including family photographs and a few of possessions of my dad's that I had to remember him by, were sealed in plastic bins. The contents of these bins were preserved because they fortuitously had been moved down into the cement basement and were now safely stowed in the back of my Jeep.

While the bin preserved good childhood memories and reassured me that I could refer back to these items whenever I missed my dad or wanted to remember my happiest youthful days, the burnt house felt like a message from the Universe that it was time to move on—something I had already felt.

I wonder now, how do we let certain things go? When we realize that we don't need to be what others expect us to be, that we don't have to do what others tell us to do, that we have choices … how does the journey change? How do our relationships change?

Where I would go after the fire, I had not yet figured out. I shifted out of park and into drive and moved toward whatever the Universe had planned for me.

PART I

DECISIONS

Ages: 0–9

June 1981–September 1990

Age 6

From the time I was adopted until I was six years old, my parents and I lived in a small ranch-style home in Concord, Rhode Island. We had a fenced-in backyard and our house was situated in front of a manufacturing plant of some kind. Its large black and yellow wooden sign was displayed in the corner of our front yard, facing the street. There was a steady amount of traffic in and out of the plant with cars and trucks kicking up dust all day long.

We lived in the suburbs, but I recall there being a jalopy helicopter residing in our backyard. Yes, a helicopter! I always grew up with strange and interesting things that most other homes did not have. To some, these could have been treasures—to others, this was junk. I'm certain that however my dad obtained these items, he didn't pay much, if anything, at all. My dad was the king of bartering. I remember him trading guns (often shotguns) in exchange for fixing someone's electrical issue (computers, radios—you name it, he could fix it).

Age 8

My hand was wrapped in gauze that covered a menacing smile of black stitches I had received just days before, after cutting my hand open on a ceramic pot. My parents led me up the walkway to a big, red barn-style house. There was clutter everywhere on the lawn as we approached the door. I could hear the sounds of talking, yelling, frenetic activity coming from inside the house as we rang the bell. Later, I surmised that this must have been a foster home.

The scratched and faded red wooden door creaked as it was pulled open and we were ushered inside. I don't remember the person who welcomed us because my senses were overpowered by the rambunctious children all around, the well-worn environment, and the smell of the home. What was it that made my nose tingle? Before I could place it, my attention was suddenly focused on the almost-three-year-old girl who was being brought into the room and directed toward my parents. As all eyes attached to all size bodies were focused on us, peeking around chairs and doorways, my mother turned to me and announced, "This is your new sister."

I knew that I was adopted but I had been an only child for eight years. What was going on? What was happening to my life? My parents were adopting another girl? I struggled to process this new information in that moment.

The very tall woman who had let us in placed both hands on the shoulders of this brown-haired girl standing in front of us. The girl's wide, frightened, dark eyes were darting back and forth between my parents and me as this stranger urged (even pushing a bit) the little girl toward my mother. "This is May," she said by way of introduction.

May was olive-toned, skinny, and fragile. With my ginger hair and blue eyes, we looked nothing alike. But May looked like my parents. My mom had a Mediterranean look—despite her French-Canadian roots—standing medium height with short, tightly permed brown hair, laughing brown eyes, and the kind of skin that tanned easily. My father was tall, with an outdoorsy build and weathered skin. It didn't occur to me then, but later I was constantly aware of how little I looked like my adoptive parents and how much my adopted sister did. Did I wonder then if they would love her more because she looked like them? Did I wonder if they wanted a new child because of something I'd done or didn't do? I don't remember. Did I eventually wish they would send her back? Absolutely.

With May's hand tucked firmly into my mother's, and me tagging along behind wondering what the heck just happened, off we went to start our big happy family life together. At least I assume that was the plan—if only that had been the case.

In addition to all the bartered clutter, our home was often surrounded by stray dogs and cats—and we just took care of them. At one point, we had rescued a blind raccoon that was hit by a car and nursed it back to health. That's how it felt to me as a child; that we rescued May the way a person rescues a dog (or raccoon). But maybe, just like my father enjoyed rescuing and repurposing mechanical things, my mother liked the concept of rescuing a child and doing good. Did she, like my dad, want a project to "fix" and "improve?"

When we got home with my new sister, my mother asked me to go for a walk. She explained, "May has 'failure to thrive.' You need to be really careful around your little sister."

"What do you mean?" I asked.

"May's mother left her as a baby and didn't give her love or food. She didn't gain weight and she's not as strong as you are. She hasn't had a real family since she was born."

"So, she can break?" I wanted to know.

My mother, ever the hero and caregiver, soothed, "We are going to get your sister strong and help her; all of us together, as a family."

Then my mother informed me, "Your sister's name is Amanda. We are going to call her Amanda. Isn't that a pretty name?"

My mother simply informed May of her new name. And, with that announcement (and some paperwork, no doubt), my sister went from being May to Amanda. She went from a foster home to my home. And my life as an only child was completely altered.

I don't think anyone asked what was right or if a name change for a toddler was appropriate. However, this *was* the mid-1980s. No one questioned my parents' modification. After all, if we could change the name of a pet adopted from a shelter, why not change the name of a child? It never occurred to me that changing a three-year-old child's name didn't make any sense. Nor did I understand the possible psychological impact and identity issues that could arise later in life. In a recent conversation with my therapist, she commented on how unusual this is and how that kind of casual attitude toward the value of a child's identity reveals my parents' lack of awareness around the repercussions of this decision.

Over the years, we found that Amanda turned out to have a lot of unexpected issues, most likely stemming from early childhood trauma, presumed abuse and neglect, subsequent separation and abandonment by her birth parents, and formative years spent in foster homes.

Despite the overwhelming evidence, I really didn't know I was living with a sister with severe mental health needs. Somewhere deep within my being, I knew she was acting her own version of "normal," but we never spoke of it. Anytime I would say anything to my parents, it did not matter how severe the situation was, "She's only a baby," would be the supplied justification for that behavior. No matter how old Amanda got, I was still hearing the same "baby" excuse.

Amanda and I had little in common and our five-year age gap seemed insurmountable. At first, I was happy to have a little sister to follow me around, but soon I realized we were just too different. I spent my time outdoors, playing sports, and on my own while Amanda craved attention and enjoyed more artsy and group activities. I imagine she was frustrated that I was out of the house most of the time. With all her extra energy, the older we got, my sister used the time that I was increasingly out of the house to intrude in my space, destroy my things, and engage in other not-so-passive aggressive behaviors. Perhaps to get my attention—perhaps just because that was who she was.

When making plans for adopting a new child, my parents decided we needed more space. When I was eight, shortly before Amanda's adoption, we moved to the opposite side of our town, where my dad built our large four-bedroom, two-and-a-half-bath colonial-style house. Previously, we had been located on a busy main street in town. The new house was built on a few acres of land at the bottom of a long and winding dirt road and surrounded by trees as far as the eye could see.

Before construction could begin on the house, they had to first clear the lot and knock down a forest of trees to make it happen. I believe my dad did the majority of this work on his own. We had backhoes, dump trucks, and all sorts of equipment on our new property for quite some time. My dad left plenty of nature around the perimeter of our property for privacy and for us to enjoy.

My parents decided they would save money building the new house by doing something unconventional. Typically, most people would use dirt or soil to smooth out land before building or landscaping, but we had truck-loads of filler from the dump brought in. It was used to level the terrain after trees and roots and underbrush were excavated. The dump material was then covered with soil, upon which my dad began to build.

The end result was a sloped 12-foot embankment running up to the left side of our house. You would pull off the main dirt road, drive up our dusty driveway, and the closer to the house you got, the farther you'd be from the land below. This embankment made for a great sledding hill growing up, as well as a place where adventures and rather dangerous youthful experiences took place.

Since this land came from the dump, all sorts of treasures could be found just beneath the dirt surface of our yard. Old coffee cans, metal toy cars, and just simple trash could easily be unearthed after a storm or with a simple trowel as we planted seasonal flowers. As a child, it was always an adventure what you might find just out the front door. Imagination could soar with wonder over where the objects came from, who owned them, or what kinds of things you could create with them.

I remember when I was around 10 years old, my cousin Julia and I were digging in the yard at the house. We were just digging to dig. Something to do because we knew we would find all sorts of fascinating items! How deep a hole could we make? Eventually, about 6 feet down, we hit the septic tank. We had gone so far down, we couldn't get ourselves out of the hole.

After our parents rescued us and gave us our strong verbal reprimands (a.k.a. "handed us our asses!") and punishment, I went back outside, found a cabinet door from the scrap heap that was the side of my house, and made a trapdoor cover over the gaping hole. We covered the door with dirt. Our family never filled in the hole—a recipe for disaster.

During construction of the house itself, as we toured the progress, I can remember the clean, fresh smell of recently cut wood and sawdust. Anytime I come across the smell of wood chips and sawdust it still signals newness, growth, and unfamiliar possibilities. It was one of the few clean childhood smells I had.

I don't remember the inside of our old ranch-style house ever being filthy, but I was also six, so that could explain the poor memory. But I do remember the yard always filled with tangled piles of metal pipes, copper wiring, and other debris. This all moved with us to the new home. My dad was big into satellite dishes. Metal pipes (sometimes 30 to 40 feet long) flanked the side of our house. To this day, I'm not sure what purpose they truly served, but I'm certain my dad had a use for it all. It was placed just off in the distance beside our hand-me-down above-ground swimming pool.

From kindergarten through fifth grade I went to a Catholic elementary school. When I was in the third grade, I was standing first in line to exit the classroom when the bishop (rarely present on campus) was visiting the school. I was at the threshold of the door to the hallway with my classmates lined up behind me when the bishop reached down and fondled my adolescent breast. Immediately, I knew it was wrong, but didn't know how to react. When I went home, I told my parents. I don't remember the outcome, but there was a meeting at the school about the incident. From that point forward, my hatred of the Church grew by the day. It was one of my first experiences of not having a "safe space"—before Amanda redefined that term for me.

The one positive thing I recall about my Catholic school experience was the janitor. Mary was older, very friendly, with big blonde 1980's hair. My parents couldn't always get me after school at the same time as the rest of the kids; no doubt due to my parents' overlapping work schedules. This necessitated me following Mary around the practically empty school watching her clean. Mary would let me walk with her from classroom to classroom as she worked, often giving me apples she found. She seemed like the only rational adult in my life who didn't expect anything of me. I needed that. She was perfectly content to have my company and I hers.

My love for softball blossomed when I was about eight years old. As I got older, softball was a great way to pass time because we had practices nearly every night and games on the weekends, sometimes multiple games in a single day. This kind of organized activity precluded me from spending much time in the house. I found myself playing on more than one team at a time, fueling my increasing need to be out of the house. I often took care of Amanda after school and I had dinner with the family (which was some combination of the four of us, but rarely all at once) if I wasn't at practice or a game.

My mother worked second shift (3 p.m. to 11 p.m.) at the hospital as a licensed practical nurse. When it was softball season, she would arrange her schedule so she could attend my softball games as often as possible. She was prone to embarrassing me with her all-out cackle of a laugh that could be heard across the entire field and random I-don't-care-what-anyone-else-thinks-or-does behaviors. I can still picture so clearly one game in high-school where my mother was trying to carry her resin lawn chair down the hill to the field to watch me play and, finally, instead of carrying it, she just threw it on the ground, gave it a push and let it roll down the hill by itself. I was on the mound about to pitch and this rolling chair and my mother's effusive arm movements totally distracted me, the spectators, and all the players. Everyone laughed. I was mortified. But that was my mother. She supported my efforts at sports whether I wanted her to or not—that's what moms do.

My mother would bring my sister sometimes. Other times, my sister would attend with my dad while my mom was at work.

When I was trying out for the 12-and-under all-star team for softball, my mother supported my sports goals by helping me practice. We were outside in our front yard where, gloveless, she was pitching me some balls. I hit a line drive straight to her face and she was knocked flat to the ground. For half a second, I was proud of the power in my hit, but then I transitioned into panic, raced over to see how my mom was, and found her covered in blood. I sped into the house to get ice and towels. The radio was playing the Top 40s, and I heard, "I'm looking in your big brown eyes." "Sweat," performed by UB40, came through the speakers before I turned around and headed back out to put ice on her eye.

I gave my mother—still lying in the grass—the ice and towel and ran to get our neighbor Donna. By the time she and I reached my mother, her face was purple, swollen, and covered in blood. Donna was visibly aghast by my mom's appearance. Refusing our neighbor's offer to help, my mother got herself into our minivan, managed to drop me off at my all-star tryouts, and then drove her bloodied self to the walk-in clinic to get looked at. My mom was tough!

Although I was still shaken at the tryouts, I made the team, despite worrying about my mom the entire time. The end result was that my mother's glasses saved her eye, but also lacerated the entire space under her eye, which needed over 20 stiches. She looked awful for months after. Every time I looked at the scar on her face, I relived that day, well into my adult years.

Age 9

When the weather cooled and the softball gear was packed away, I would physically carry large pieces of wood, loading them in a trailer to be driven to our basement window. We had a wood-burning stove and chopped down our own trees to heat our home. Sometimes I hated it, but most times I relished being out of the house and away from my screaming sister and mother. I got to spend time with my father. He didn't talk much. He was a man of activity, so I was a girl of activity.

I remember spending much of my youth riding my mini-bike, shooting guns, or doing an array of other physical activities—like shooting a bow with real arrows, riding in a go-cart we borrowed from my dad's friend, and then deciding to build our own go-cart that oddly resembled a coffin. I was always outside and so was my dad. I certainly was not a delicate girl, more like the epitome of a tomboy.

In 1990 I had my first crush. Miss Parante was my fourth-grade science teacher. At the time I didn't know it was a crush. I loved everything about being around her and being in her class—perhaps it was more of an infatuation.

Despite my normal distaste for school and studying, for Miss Parante, I worked hard. I was awarded with some kind of recognition in Miss Parante's class during the winter semester. My mom wanted to get me a special gift to celebrate this school-based accomplishment (as they were rare), so off we went on a mother/daughter trip to Kmart. I normally hated shopping, but this was a chance to get my mother to myself and I was promised that we would not be shopping for clothing, thankfully (I hated clothes shopping and, admittedly, still do). The closest Kmart was a solid 30-minute drive from where we lived, so going two towns over to Walden was often a production, even though it was the city where my mom worked.

At the Kmart, I got to select what I wanted. I requested a slushy in a cool Red Sox plastic cup and a mini-basketball (all the rage back then). On the drive home I stared out the window, envisioning the playing time I would have with the new basketball at home. We had a homemade basketball hoop on the back of our garage where I spent hours alone shooting hoops regardless of the weather.

It had been lightly snowing when we had set out but began to snow rather heavily as we were heading home. There were two main routes from Walden to our house, both of which required crossing Grayson's Pond. The pond spans a significant part of Concord. Regardless of which route you took, there were minor bridges to cross. My mom preferred the Route 9 way home, which was a much more winding road than the straight shot of Route 114.

As we drove down Route 9 and turned onto the small and twisting road toward the bridge, I could sense my mother starting to panic. At this point in our journey, we couldn't see anything ahead except pure white massive snow coming down. Our wipers were at full speed, but it didn't seem to improve our visibility. I was sitting up straight and gripping the door armrest. I became afraid of us driving off the bridge and ending up in the pond.

My fear of ending up in the pond was rational because my mother had a phobia about bridges. Every year, during our annual pilgrimage to my dad's family in Pennsylvania, my mother would shriek in panic crossing the Tappan Zee Bridge. I was acutely aware of my mom's fear; I could feel it invade the car as the snowstorm blanketed our car in whiteness. Our minivan slowed to a crawl. We did not have snow tires or chains installed despite being in New England and knowing better.

As we were creeping up the road to the narrow Grayson's Pond bridge, my mom, her voice trembling a little, asked me, "Jenn, what should we do?

Should we cross this bridge or go the other way?" It almost sounded like she was talking to herself, but she directed it at me. I thought, "Why is she asking me? I'm nine years old!?" And yet, despite not having ever driven, somehow wise beyond my years about this, I offered my opinion, "If we turn around and go up Route 114, it will take longer but we would be on a shorter and wider bridge and I don't think we would have a problem."

"I agree. We'll go that way." My mother turned the car around cautiously. We straightened out and headed back toward the safer route, and it was in that moment that I realized I was already an adult in our relationship. I would bear the responsibility of decision-making for many choices our family needed to make in the future. Contemplating this new awareness—part proud, part nervous—I guided the car home with my mind as my mother white-knuckle gripped the steering wheel and leaned in toward the windshield to focus on getting us home safely.

PART II

DEVASTATION

Ages: 11-15

September 1992–May 1997

Age 11

When we were younger, my sister and I were dropped off after school at the hospital where my mother worked. We sat in the nurses' lounge eating snacks (my favorites were hospital staples—Keebler Club Crackers, ginger ale, and crushed ice in Styrofoam cups), doing homework, coloring, and playing games while we waited for my dad to pick us up.

When we moved houses, I changed schools. Having reached the sixth grade, I was entrusted to get off the bus on my own and stay home alone with my sister until my dad got home.

We had secret spots around the outside of the house where we would hide the house key. If someone forgot to leave me a key, I would crawl through the dining room window over the basement bulkhead to get in the house. I left it unlocked so I knew I could get in. I don't know if my parents or my sister ever knew I did this. It was one of the survival strategies I employed because I often felt like it was up to me to ensure I was taken care of.

For a short window of time, my mother's mother, Meme, lived with us in our new house before she was moved into a nursing home as she slowly lost her battle against Alzheimer's. She had the larger bedroom down the hallway from the rest of the bedrooms. When Meme moved out, I got her bigger room—and more space to myself.

I loved those afternoons at the hospital because the hospital was so clean and pure, while our home was cluttered, sloppy, and dirty. I don't remember exactly when I realized how bad my home appeared to other people. Had it gotten worse as I got older or was it always that way? I was embarrassed to have friends from school come to my house. Not every room in our house looked like a hoarder lived there but many of them did. The majority of the house was disorganized, dirty, and smelled of animal urine. We weren't able to find anything we needed.

My mom would wash our clothes and then dump the baskets of clean laundry on her bedroom floor. Four humans' clothes all piled into one heap meant you had to rummage like you were digging through the dump to find the shirt you were looking for or the socks you needed for the day. I don't remember a time when our clothes weren't heaped into a wrinkled pile on their floor. I probably was assigned the job of sorting and folding laundry, or maybe other chores, but I was a typical tween and likely didn't listen

My dad worked as an electrician in Princeton, about 45 minutes from our house. After Meme moved out, since my parents worked opposite shifts, each day I would have between 2:30 p.m. and 5 p.m., roughly, to be home without supervision.

Despite having free rein and the ability to do whatever I pleased, I never took advantage of this to do things that were illegal like others might have. I did do some foolish things, like trying to chip ice in the frozen pool and falling in when no one was home. I rescued myself and used a blow dryer to defrost, but my father came home and figured out what had happened. I have no recollection of the disciplinary action I was given, but I'm sure there was something.

The one area I admit to taking advantage of having no supervision was in the kitchen. It was during these fend-for-yourself times that I developed poor eating habits. Once I got home from school, I would often sit down in front of the TV and eat oatmeal creme pies or a bag of popcorn, drink soda, and devour anything else I could get my hands on in the hours I had alone. Since we lived far from a grocery store, we did our bulk shopping in Walden, which meant I had access to warehouse-sized quantities of food.

I never ate at school. I was anxious about eating a meal in front of people. To this day, I am unclear from where this anxiety stemmed. An added anxiety was the need to have a coat or sweater on at all times—heavy in the winter or light in the summer, it didn't matter what season. Perhaps there was something about the fear of exposing myself to others that still follows me to this day in needing to keep on layers of clothing, even in the heat (something currently on my *To Tackle* list in therapy).

In school, oftentimes, I would use my lunch money to buy Skittles and Twix from the candy machine in the cafeteria and I would quietly eat them when no one was around. I didn't know how to eat healthy or what eating healthy even meant. Sugar became my trusted companion.

My mom, a great chef in her own mind, would cook dinner and leave it for us before she left for work. What we actually ate when my dad got home was a combination of what she had left for us and then other snack foods if her preparations weren't tolerable. Fortunately, my level of physical activity counterbalanced all my poor eating habits and my weight was not an issue.

In the sixth grade when I moved to the new school, my new friend Erica and I became instant best friends. Her parents were divorced and lived on opposite ends of town, so when Erica was being driven from one parent to the other, it was easy to stop in the middle and pick me up or drop me off. I started to spend a lot of time in Erica's homes.

I'm unsure where Amanda spent much of her time while I was away. I assume also spending time at a friend's house or perhaps being by one of my parents' sides.

Since Erica's homes were as dysfunctional as mine in their own unique ways, I wasn't embarrassed when she came to my house to play or study. We seemed to spend every waking moment together when I wasn't playing sports. And we did all the sorts of things newly teenage adolescents do (and then some) because we were unsupervised 99% of the time.

When Erica and I were in either of her houses, we were likely alone for a good part of the time or her parents were distracted. Erica's mother owned a chocolate shop in Walden (the same town where my mother worked), about 45 minutes away from their house. She had retail hours. Erica's father, like mine, was a tradesman with standard 9 to 5 hours.

Erica's mother had remarried and her stepfather, from my perspective, was an angry alcoholic. My mother was also an alcoholic. We could relate to the dance one does to not irritate the inebriated! The one redeeming thing about this man, to me at the time, was that he had a boat and would take us out on open ocean water for day trips.

When Erica's father remarried, his new wife moved in with her severely autistic son, Matthew, Erica's stepbrother. The couple spent much of their time and energy on Matthew, much the way my parents were attentive to Amanda. Matthew needed constant attention as he was nonverbal and reactive to everything sensory. We were noisy, giggling girls shut away on our own in Erica's bedroom or outside exploring.

What do girls who are unattended do when they're teenagers? We ate what we wanted, skipped school sometimes, and traveled by bus wherever we pleased. We would sneak back to my house after pretending to go to school and sit around all day calling 800 numbers. My mom worked second shift, but had the occasional day shift, so we would have the house to ourselves and planned our skip days accordingly. I had a fascination with advertising, starting in the sixth grade, and we'd call to get free samples, order brochures, participate in surveys, etc. It was free to call, so why would I get in trouble?

I had a lime green steamer trunk with metal latches. It was the kind of thing everyone had in their rooms at the time. Because of my sister's penchant for taking all things belonging to me, I needed something with a strong lock. I don't know where I got my trunk—probably something my father found for me—but in that trunk, I kept the brochures for bed and breakfast inns that we called. I added samples of nuts, lotions, make-up, tampons, soup mixes, even Depends pads, and more. If it was free, we ordered it. Since I brought in the family mail after school each day, no one got suspicious.

I loved the travel brochures for all sorts of exotic destinations and collected them by the dozens. I could imagine myself leaving my cluttered, anxiety-producing home and visiting resorts with peaceful beaches, gorgeous views, and lots of entertaining activities. No sister. No yelling parents. Instead of foul animal odors, I fantasized about gardens with florals wafting to my open-windowed room. Of course, I then ended up on marketing mailing lists and the mailbox overflowed with all kinds of junk daily—all addressed to me.

When Erica and I got bored with the 800 numbers (nothing new or interesting to acquire), we started to call 900 numbers. Now this *was* a problem. I think we called every day for a month at 99 cents per minute. I don't blame my parents for their fury now because that bill must have been HUGE! And because of that behavior, my dad whooped my butt with a paddle that was a half inch of solid pine wood. Another time, he pulled out his leather belt. It wasn't often that I got beaten but when I pushed my parents to the very limits of their tolerance, it did happen, and it was intense.

Erica and I would stay up at all hours watching the local greyhound racing. When we couldn't be together, we would watch together over the phone. The greyhounds always had cool names like Lucky Lady, Show-Gun Spirit, Win-Lose-or-Draw. Our 11-year-old minds found the dogs to be clever, and it was entertaining to make bets on the races. I had a whole notebook of races where we tracked and kept score against one another. The day's races began rebroadcasting at 1 a.m. and went until 3 a.m. I watched the greyhound racing religiously for years.

Erica and I would buy joke books from the Scholastic Book Fairs at school. I kept them around to make myself laugh and smile when stuff at home with my sister got to be too much. Every day with Amanda there was either something stolen or an argument that caused friction and chaos within our home. I went back to these books when I was recovering from my parents' punishments. I learned to take care of my own well-being because I felt like I was not being nurtured by anyone else. Joke books became my self-care decades before that term became popular.

By default, my dad became the neighborhood handyman. He helped everyone and I believe he enjoyed it. He would barter more "stuff" in exchange for his help. I know he went across the street often to help fix things for our neighbor Maggie and her partner.

This was my first experience of seeing two adult women living together. At the time, Erica and I were attached at the hip, so the thought of living together as adults was appealing to both of us, despite not fully understanding that these two women were in a romantic relationship. I had minimal context for romantic relationships in general and the thought never entered my mind that two women could be intimate.

My dad spent a lot of time with them. I feel like he must have known they were gay, but people do live in their own bubble. I've always wondered a) Did he know they were gay? b) Did he know I was gay? c) Could the women recognize a fellow lesbian in me? d) Did that ever come up in conversation?

In hindsight, by around the time I was 10 or 12, it felt really obvious that I was gay. But my dad had a close-minded upbringing. I never got to tell him I was gay, so I have no idea what his reaction would have been.

Age 12

Despite being in a nondiverse small-minded town, I think I was raised in a household where my differences and quirks were accepted, at least to my recollection. I had many oddball-child moments that I'm sure made my parents wonder about me.

To my parents, maybe my differences were tiny and less troublesome compared to my sister's complicated behaviors. She demanded more attention than I did. I was extremely independent and self-sufficient from an early age after not having much choice in the matter.

Visibly, I looked different from the other kids in my school. Blue eyes with red hair is not a common combination. Throw in the disarray of my house and yard thanks to my parents, the collection of animals around our home, the lack of supervision by either of my parents, my penchant for playing sports versus playing with dolls, my affection for guns and shooting, riding a dirt bike, and … well yeah, I was not the average neighborhood girl.

Then, there is the fact that my sister and I were adopted. This was not as common in the 1980s and 1990s as it is now. I always knew I was adopted. I don't know when I found out, but I don't remember ever *not* knowing. My mom would proudly tell everyone about how lucky she was to have adopted. At school, we had an assignment to write out our family tree. I recall adding all the names of the people I knew about and, as I listed them, recognizing that I had nothing in common with anyone. With red hair, blue eyes, and pale skin I looked different than everyone in my household and my extended family. I felt like I saw the world in a completely different way than my family around me. It was an energetic, deep-down, soul knowledge that I was not related to these people on my family tree.

The first time I had a gut reaction to my origins was during a routine visit to the school library to take out books. Up until this point, I took it upon myself to correct anyone who struggled to pronounce my last name (informing them that it was Ukrainian) in a very direct way.

But this time, as the school librarian was checking out my books, she wondered aloud about the ethnicity of my last name, not the pronunciation, but the origin. I brusquely responded, "My name is Ukrainian. But," I added adamantly, "I'm not Ukrainian!" This time felt different, like I had to defend my heritage, while simultaneously shaking any associations to a Ukrainian name. Being adopted was very matter of fact for me. I turned and exited the library with my books, secure in having defended my DNA and heritage, despite only knowing I was some combination of Irish, Scottish, and English.

My mom had a strong Rhode Island accent, which made her sound unintelligent to me even though she wasn't. I've always felt that the Rhode Island accent is rough. Imagine a stereotypical Boston accent that is often made fun of in movies—now magnify that, and that's the accent I wanted no part of. From an early age, I was subconsciously working on disconnecting my essence from my family's. My parents were not uneducated. Both had Associate's Degrees. My mother was a nurse. My father was an electrician. He created, built, and fixed just about anything—a trait I picked up from him.

And yet, at such a young age (middle school maybe), I arrogantly thought I was smarter in different ways than my family around me. I could feel, know, and sense things that no one else saw. I felt nothing negative toward anyone else (or myself) for being different than I was, but I paradoxically still wanted my accent to not sound like where I was from.

I consciously worked on neutralizing my accent. To this day, people most often think I'm from Ohio or somewhere in the middle of the country, even though I no longer care if people know I'm from Rhode Island. I'm not hiding anymore, but as a public speaker and consultant, it has been beneficial to sound geographically neutral to connect with my audiences and it has made it easier for people to understand me. So, I suppose there's an upside to all of this.

Age 13

In seventh grade, one of my classmate's last names, which began with a B, was changed to a W mid-year when his mother got remarried. Therefore, his homeroom changed, and he was now in homeroom alongside Erica and me. Our last names began with T and R.

This boy began taunting Erica and me, calling us lesbians. We were adolescents and our hormones were beginning to stir; boys and girls around us were looking at things differently. At the time, I had no idea what a lesbian was. This was the early 1990s (three to four years before Ellen DeGeneres publicly came out) and lesbians weren't talked about. It wasn't a thing seen on TV or in magazines and movies.

My life as a contrarian started young, so if everyone else was into something, I wanted nothing to do with it. This didn't help my lack of data points, so I had no idea what being a lesbian actually meant. I understood more when the taunting got worse and he would announce to the class that Erica and I were in love and that we kissed. It was typical middle school bullying that escalated quickly, but, fortunately, was isolated to just middle school.

At the time, I didn't identify with anything W was saying. Though Erica and I were in each other's space all the time, I never had a crush on her. We were typical teenage best friends.

In hindsight, my adult mind can look back at this experience and objectively see that W must have been going through a lot at home and was projecting his anger onto Erica and me. Meanwhile, Erica and I were both coping with our complex home lives and had enough to deal with without worrying about a bully and his baggage.

At the time, I, like my classmates, had superficial crushes on boys in my grade. I don't know if they were legit crushes or if I did it because everyone else did. I had no desire to kiss a boy (or a girl). I just wasn't interested.

I recall my first kiss in the second grade. I was seven when a hockey player named Peter kissed me on the cheek in school. We were boyfriend/girlfriend for a little while. For Valentine's Day, he gave me a snow globe that said, "Meant to be." I bought him, at the supermarket, a sticker book and a full set of hockey stickers to put in the book. True love!

To be honest, I had really only had one love; that was playing softball.

In 1997, Ellen DeGeneres came out as a lesbian. I didn't watch the television show *Ellen* or really remember the hubbub of her coming out, despite it being huge news at the time. I believe I was oblivious to anything outside of softball and I was in survival mode at home.

In ninth grade, I began reading Ellen's book *My Point ... And I Do Have One*. I don't know what prompted me to purchase it or quite honestly where I even bought it or acquired the money to buy it? My parents? Myself? Library? Truly no idea. That book struck me as one of the funniest things I had ever read (and I did enjoy a good knock-knock joke book). I remember crying, I was laughing so hard. Looking back, I do not know if my young self knew Ellen DeGeneres was gay and subconsciously picked up that book for that reason. Regardless, I thought Ellen was a brilliant comedian regardless of her sexual orientation.

I did not experience the common conflicted childhood struggles of knowing you were gay but not knowing what to do with that information and suffering through teenage years in silence. I kept my head down, focused on sports, and was choosing between fight or flight within my home on a daily basis. Maybe if I hadn't been constantly responding to trauma at home for most of my youth, I would have picked up on being gay sooner? Hindsight is an interesting thing.

Because of my parents' occasional overlapping schedules, I would be responsible for the house, my sister, and taking care of myself. Despite the rarity of all four of us being in the house at once, "home" was a hostile environment. My parents fought. A lot. I don't really remember the roots or the reason for their fighting or what it was ever about. I tried to mediate often but it would end up with my mom drunkenly slamming her dinner plate or sending it sailing across the kitchen table and my dad retreating to his man cave in the basement.

The tension with my parents increasingly grew. Shortly after she came to live with us, I instinctively knew something wasn't right with Amanda. But I was eight, who was I to say if something was off? As time went on, Amanda acted out more, and I often told my parents that I thought something was wrong with her. They never listened to me. Why would they listen to their 12-year-old canary in a coal mine? They probably thought I was being dramatic, trying to get attention. Or they were so preoccupied with earning income and managing their two work schedules that if no one got hurt at home, everything else could wait.

But Amanda was not one to be ignored. If my parents weren't around to pay attention, she would break everything I owned. It was always chalked up as an accident, but I knew it wasn't. I knew it was intentional. I would tell my parents that she had just broken whatever item, and they would reply with their signature phrase, "She's only a baby." Amanda would look at me, a certain smug way, a child's way of saying, "Ha ha, sucker!" It would confirm what I had already known—she was operating maliciously. It's hard to fathom such a young child operating with malice, but if you've seen it and/or experienced it, you know the look.

Then Amanda began stealing my things and, once again, I looked like the dramatic one, as if I had misplaced my things and was just looking to place blame.

Amanda did odd, innocuous things like spend hours sitting on the couch humming and rocking back and forth or banging her head against the back of the couch. Or she would constantly eat, as if she didn't have a shut-off switch. She would hide food under her bed—cans of cupcake frosting, bowls of salad, sandwiches, anything really. One would have thought that my mother, a nurse, would have picked up on these clues of burgeoning mental health needs and taken steps to get help for her child sooner rather than later. But I recognize now that my mom was likely doing the best she could, given her circumstances.

The thing my young mind saw that no one else did was Amanda's ability to manipulate any situation. She was able to manipulate my parents like it was her job. She would go to one, ask for something, and get a *no* answer. Then she'd go to the other, ask the same question, and get a *yes* answer. Unlike typical children, who do this and are grateful to have gotten away with whatever it was, she would make sure both of my parents knew what the other said after the fact. She wanted the arguing. She wanted the chaos. Most kids would white lie or manipulate to get their way and be done with it, but she wanted more. She wanted the tension in the house and for all of us to be at odds. It worked. We were.

Amanda and I never fully got along. I tried for a long time, assuming I had to be the more mature one since I was five years older. Since I was the one taking care of her after school, I believed she was supposed to listen to me. Unfortunately, she did not agree. And my parents were nowhere around to mediate or lay down the law.

As I got older and smarter, when hiding things in the garage, closets, drawers, or under beds was no longer working, I began guarding my stuff with any tools I could find. I was making sure my sister was not allowed anywhere near my room or my belongings. I went so far as to change the lock on my bedroom door. I swapped out the standard bath and closet doorknob for one that had a pinhole lock. I was excited because my room was finally safe and locked. It didn't take long before Amanda realized she could stick any small screwdriver (or object) into the knob and pop it open. I was enraged and upset. I would yell, "She got into my room again!" Only to be met with, "She's only a baby," by one of my parents.

Eventually, this breaking and entering was too much and I upgraded to a front door keyed-entry lock and added a dead bolt. This may have been the beginning of my handy(wo)man skill development, as this required me to take the door off the hinges, drill a 3-inch hole, and then rehang the door. I needed this to keep Amanda from getting into my room when I was outside and to keep me safe and away from her when I was home and wanted privacy. It didn't take long before she had broken into my room again—and stolen more things. And my parents did nothing.

I began to resign myself to the fact that nothing was safe in my house. I had no safe space that was my own. I became a master locksmith, constantly finding new ways to deadbolt my bedroom door to keep Amanda out. If you can imagine a big city urban apartment with four deadbolts and sliding chains, that's what my rural country home bedroom door looked like. But there was still no keeping her out.

On the rare occasion that I forgot to lock my door, I would immediately regret it. I would return home to find money missing or possessions broken.

Somewhere inside me I was hoping she would change. I was hoping that one day I wouldn't have to worry about theft or vandalism in my own home.

I don't know if it was conscious that I would leave the door unlocked from time to time or if it was a pure accident, but my body would react dramatically the moment I discovered something new broken or stolen. Within seconds I was incensed.

My sister was old enough to know this behavior wasn't right. Old enough to face consequences, of which there were none because *she was just a baby.* What incentive would she have to stop? If she was trying to get my parents' attention, they weren't falling for it. It was more fun for her to keep taunting me. I was giving her the reaction she wanted. Like a vampire feeds on blood, she was feeding on my anger and frustration.

I would spend hours on end finding new ways to organize baseball cards I had been collecting since I was very young. I would put them in alphabetical order by last name, by team, by brand, by year. You name it and I found another way to organize them over and over again. I was the same with many other things I collected like Pez dispensers and those tiny plastic baseball and football helmets from the grocery store 25-cent machine. I would sort and arrange those things as well. My room was my sanctuary despite its lack of security or safety. I made it work the best I could, given the chaos around me.

I couldn't fall asleep at night unless my closets were clean and the closet doors were closed—more controlling what I could. Being in our house felt like being in a prison. I would spend my days outside or holed up in my room away from everyone else with a door full of locks.

Anytime I had friends in my house I became a soldier escorting a VIP through a war zone area. Before we entered, I'd warn my guest of the situation.

"We're going to enter the foyer. You'll see stairs ahead of you. Don't look down the hallway. Ignore the smells and don't step in the cat puke! Just follow my lead."

Then, as I opened the door, "Ready?" and warned, "Hold your nose!"

We'd enter and my hands would push from behind, aiming for the staircase, while I would chant, "Go, go, go, go!" as we raced up the stairs.

At the top of the stairs, I'd direct them, "Turn left into my room," and I'd shut the door like someone was chasing us.

"Whew. We made it through without incident!" I would think gratefully, as I smiled, gesturing, directing my friend's view around my room, like a model on "The Price is Right," showing off the prizes behind Door #2. We had made it to my room where I had candles burning to mask the odors vaporing in from under the doorframe.

In my room, my friends could see that I wasn't the dirty one. I wasn't the problem. As my guests entered my immaculate room, I felt redemption. In my room, there was a place for everything and everything was in its place—except when it was stolen.

Every single day living with Amanda was filled with fear—what would she do next? I was living the true definition of sleeping with one eye open—another pattern I repeated into adulthood. What would she steal of mine? How would she try to hurt me? One of the really low points in this battle with my sister happened when she had pushed me too far, had smirked just once too often, and had stolen something very personal and precious to me.

Despite Amanda having grown taller than me, one day I used all my strength, grabbed my sister's throat, and pushed her against the wall at the top of the stairs, lifting her off the ground. I could have easily tossed her down the stairs. I could have cut off her breathing and killed her. My eyes were hard and narrowed, my hands strong and determined. This was my "do NOT fuck with me anymore, LITTLE sister!" moment.

The adrenaline in my fight response reaction was enough to send her whimpering away. I don't remember exactly what triggered me so deeply or why it happened on that particular day. It may have been a build-up of just biting my tongue too many times. I often felt that ignoring the behavior and situation would make it easier or go away faster, but occasionally even the calmest lake will churn before a storm.

I wish I could say that experience changed her, but in actuality, it did nothing in the long run except cause me to fear who I was becoming by staying in our home.

Age 14

It aggravated me that I had to walk around with a janitor-style set of keys to get in and out of my own bedroom even for simple things like getting a glass of water from the kitchen. Most angsty teenagers have the safe space of their bedroom and/or the security of a compassionate family. I had neither. All attention and all eyes were on my sister's increasingly bad behavior, but in the same vein, no matter what I was accusing her of that particular day, no one cared or listened to my grievances.

Like attracts like, so my circle of friends growing up all had similarly tumultuous home lives. A few friends were the products of a messy divorce, others were products of the foster care system living with a revolving door of strangers, others the product of a single parent living in Section 8 housing. Somehow, we all found each other and became a pack. This is all information I put together in hindsight, not something I realized at the time—and I don't think any of my friends did then (or perhaps even now).

At 14, Erica and I mutually decided our families were better off without us and we could fend for ourselves, out on our own, more so than in our dysfunctional home lives. When Erica and I decided to run away, it seemed like we had devised a perfect plan. I bought a brand-new hunter green Mead one-subject notebook for the occasion. I couldn't stand the chaos I grew up with at home, so I was meticulous and detail-oriented about many things. Our runaway plan was certainly one of them.

In the back of my new notebook I had written a multi-page list of supplies we needed to survive. Things such as sleeping bags, tents, something to carry water, toilet paper, food, a walking stick, etc. Our list was very specific and very granular, so it wasn't just toilet paper, but it was two-ply Scott bath tissue.

In the front of the book we had our route planned. Since we were starting from my house (which was in the middle of the woods and on the far end of town), we had quite a way to go before we even got to the main route that would take us to our destination. Where *did* we want to go was the question?

Erica and I planned to take our bikes for our escape. With limited adult supervision and free rein to do whatever we wanted, we typically got ourselves wherever we wanted to go via bicycle. We would easily ride 12 miles in a day. If we wanted to control our own lives, our own destiny, we could get where we wanted to but knew we needed to pack economically, so we could carry everything on our bikes without getting injured.

At one point, during our bicycling adventures around town, Erica had been so careless, not paying attention while riding her bike, that she swerved to pick up the newly acquired Derek Jeter poster she dropped and came face-to-face with a truck barreling down at her with the driver's hand planted on the horn. That scared the crap out of us. And yet, here we were, planning a trip on bicycles anyway.

Knowing our runaway plan was in the works, I paid attention to our car's odometers when running errands with either parent. I clocked and recorded the mileage to our planned checkpoints, so we could calculate how long it would take us to get there.

Our first checkpoint was Larry's on the opposite side of town, which was a small local chain that sold an array of random goods. I logged that it was 8.5 miles across town. We determined that if we were on foot it would take us an entire day to get there. How we calculated that it would take us a full day to walk 8.5 miles is a mystery. This calculation was made pre-Internet, but a current Google Map estimates our journey would have been about a six-hour walk.

Our second marked checkpoint was in Walden, two towns away, but then our plan ended. The flaws in our planning came to light. We had a route to get out of town, we had a detailed list of everything we needed, and we had the dates set, but we had no target destination.

Before we had totally given up on our plan, my parents found my runaway notebook. I had left it in my bedroom, but alas, Amanda got in and shared her discovery with them. I remember my parents being shocked. My mother already had a drink or two in her when I walked into the house to find her sitting in her recliner with my organizing notebook in her lap. First, she yelled into the air, "William, she's home!" Then she looked at me through narrowed eyes, the way a mama bear looks at a hunter coming near her cubs, and yelled, "What is this?" holding up my notebook. And, before I could respond, "Were you planning a trip? Were you leaving?"

Holding the notebook and her glass, she struggled to get herself out of the chair and asked, "Why would you want to leave? Don't you love me? Don't you care about your family?"

And then my father entered the room, "Jenn! This is very disappointing! We want an explanation!"

I defended myself and tried to (unsuccessfully) pull off the fully justified attitude, "Nobody here listens to me anyway. What difference does it make if I leave? I am invisible in this house." Sounding petulant and whiny instead of assured, I continued, "All you care about is Amanda. Everything is about Amanda. No matter what I tell you she does to me, you always take her side … "

My dad cut me off. "Your sister needs our attention. You are strong and independent." My mother blurted as she sniffled and started to cry, "I just want you to show us some love. You're never home anyway. Why would you even need to run away? You never want to spend any time with us." And my father ended the conversation with a firm, "Go to your room. Your mother and I will discuss your punishment and let you know how we're going to deal with this. You could have been killed. It's dangerous out there!"

I muttered under my breath as I left the room, "Yeah, it's dangerous in here too!"

Fall always brought about mixed emotions. I loved fall. The crispness of the air, the beautiful change in colors. But the end of fall ushers in winter. On a rainy, late fall day, I just couldn't take my mother's drunken ranting at my father's lack of reaction any longer. My peacemaking attempts—rebuffed yet again—sent me to the edge of the proverbial cliff. Erica and I had officially bagged our runaway plans and I decided it was time to be on my own anyway. Dreading the idea of being locked in the house the entire coming winter, I walked out the front door into the rainy darkness of night with only the clothes on my back.

Unlike my normally organized self, I impulsively fled without a plan. I walked up our dirt road and out to the lightly traveled main street. I passed multiple friends' houses, but it was dark, raining, and felt too late to knock on their doors (this was pre-cell phone days). I made it maybe a mile before I realized this was a futile effort and turned around to go back toward my home.

I had been gone for long enough that I assumed my parents would be looking for me, so I figured if I cut through the woods and they didn't see me I could inflict more pain on them and make them worry more.

I approached the side of our house from the woods and looked disgustedly at the piles of scrap metal that flanked the base of my home. I hunkered down, already fully soaked, under a tree that shielded the majority of water from hitting me. I was wet and freezing and had been outside for a good couple of hours at this point.

Muttering to myself, I pledged that I wouldn't be the same as my parents. "I don't know what I want to be or what I will do or where I will end up, but I will NOT live like this when I get out of here!"

The chilling rain hit my head and face and I shuddered. I pictured the clutter all over the house and determined, "I will NOT live in clutter and filth as an adult.

"I won't allow myself to be around screaming. I won't surround myself with alcoholics. I will live in a safe environment where I don't have to worry about my things being broken or stolen." I listed promises I was making to my adult self. I was going to get out and do better and be better.

Eventually, figuring my parents had enough punishment and worry, I resigned to go back into the house. So, hours after I stormed off in the dark of night, I walked back in the front door, tail between my legs, passed my family sitting in front of the television without seeming to have a care that I had been gone, and went right up into my bedroom without saying a word to anyone.

In that moment, I vowed that as soon as I was able to break free from this life, I would. A vow that remained in the front of mind until I finally broke free at 19 years old.

When my runaway plan with Erica fell apart and my solo running away did nothing, I spent solitary time in my bedroom pondering the big questions. Was the family I was born into a better fit for me than my adopted family? Was I adopted by the wrong family? How could this be my life? I didn't think or look like anyone in my house. I didn't behave like anyone in my family. It felt like I wasn't living my own life. But what was the life I thought I was meant to live? With whom was I supposed to live? Would the world have been better off without me? Teenage angst—it's a painful thing. My mother promised she would support me in finding my birth mother when I turned 18 if it was what I still wanted at the time.

I went through a depressive phase at some point shortly after the running away experience. This could have been the product of raging teenage hormones, but I remember dubbing "The World I Know" by Collective Soul as my suicide song. If I were to kill myself, it would somehow include that song. I would hear *it* and immediately get my fix of depressing soul music.

My despair was a combination of so many things. My self-determined standard was to be perfect, so if I couldn't be perfect, I didn't feel like I belonged. By the way, this did not apply to my grades in school. I was a mostly C-student, with an occasional B here and there throughout high school. The fact that I went on to get an undergraduate and graduate degree, graduating summa cum laude, is a surprise to many who knew me back then.

I always felt like my life was slightly out of focus, but I was never able to pinpoint exactly why. How can you fix something you can't identify? During my angsty teenage years, I remember thinking, "The worst that can happen is that I kill myself." This is not a great mindset, but it was a fleeting thought that would cross my mind from time to time. It sounds morbid, but I looked at the suicide option as the ultimate test of one's will, one's endurance, one's commitment to live a bigger and bolder life. I began to feel that if you know the worst-case scenario is that you kill yourself, then you literally have nothing to lose, so there's no reason you shouldn't go all-in, all the time.

There were enough instances where this string of thoughts during these dark times as a teenager really made sense to me. I never truly thought I would act on it, but it was something that crossed my mind often enough that it spooked me.

At some point, my sister began having doctor appointments quite a distance from our home. Presumably these were visits to specialists we didn't have in our town. I was dragged along, but I had no idea why we were there or what we were doing. I remember some of the doctors' offices being a good 45 minutes from the house in a direction we rarely went, which, at the time, felt like an eternity. I didn't care and I didn't pay attention. On the visits I was dragged to, I would just sit in the waiting room with a puzzle book or some Tiger handheld electronic game to keep me occupied. These were the visits I remember. I have no idea how many other appointments Amanda had where I wasn't involved because I was playing sports or at Erica's house. I suspect there were many.

By the time I was around 14, my parents were discussing divorce. I don't remember the specifics, but my dad had moved into the spare bedroom. By early 1997, when I was 15, my dad had moved into his own apartment and fled our house, much as I wished for myself. This seemed to have triggered my sister's behavior to worsen. Without both parents under one roof to manipulate for her benefit, she had become insufferable to live with.

When raising a challenging child occupies your marriage, some marriages come closer together and get stronger, while others break apart. In our case, our family had physically broken apart. But this was just the beginning.

Age 15

The older we got, the more out of control my mother's drinking became. She drank every day. I began to see that my parents' fights were now centered around how much my mom was drinking. My dad would make statements like, "Kathleen, I'm not doing this." And then he would go into his basement man cave, his safe space from the chaos.

Our kitchen, like many, was set up with the appliances on one side and the dining area opposite. We had a buffet and a hutch on the side of the room. My mother would hide her wine in the hutch. She bought the largest size (a gallon) of Carlo Rossi Rhine wine. When we were having company over or my mother had been getting more out of hand than usual and I wanted to rein her in, I would take the bottle of wine and pour it down the sink. I hoped it would keep my mother from becoming too embarrassing.

Day by day, night by night, my mother would sit in her tattered, old recliner in the family room and drink. Prior to passing out during warmer months, we would sit and enjoy watching the Red Sox play. I remember summer nights with the windows open, ushering in the smell of fresh air versus the stench we had otherwise. I cherished the early evening good times, because after a certain point, she would fall asleep or pass out in the chair with her head lolling against the handmade afghans covering the back. She would snore lightly with her mouth open. Some days, I just thought she was pathetic and felt bad for her. Other days, I would look at her in disgust. I wanted to shove things in her open mouth until she couldn't breathe so she'd wake up and realize she was ignoring her family. Instead, I just kept destroying her wine, a futile endeavor.

I would typically pour out the contents of the large wine bottles into the sink. But if I was in a rage and felt out of control, I would smash the whole jug of wine in the sink. I made sure to do this while my mother was awake, so she knew I was destroying something she loved.

It seemed that no matter how I got rid of the inflammatory liquid, how much I tried to control my mother's behavior, my mother would go buy more the next day. If she was drunk to the point of being about to pass out, she wouldn't have been drinking much more anyway so my "statement" had zero effect. My actions, even when recognized, only impacted that one night's drinking, and yet I kept repeating this same pointless behavior. In the grand scheme of things, I cost my mother's budget $8.99 for each gallon she had to replace.

In our town there were three liquor stores she frequented. My mother would alternate which store she went to. This rotation was designed for my mother's ego. No one store clerk would see her every few days, so the rationalization was that it wouldn't look so bad if she only came in for the wine every week or so, right?

I had a love-hate relationship with taking these trips with her. I didn't always go, but when I did, I would be treated with a Slim Jim, beef jerky, or a packet of sunflower seeds as my reward for going on the wine replenishment trips.

I had made my Catholic Confirmation on April 29, a Tuesday, where we took a full family picture. I was miserable about making my confirmation because I was anti-religion and it shows in the portrait. While the bishop was anointing me and I was supposedly becoming an adult in the eyes of the Church, I was replaying a "movie scene" in my head of when I was groped by a bishop in the third grade. I was filled with loathing. The Church should have been a safe place for a young girl, but it wasn't.

Two days after the confirmation ceremony, while my mother was at work, my dad dropped my sister and me back to our house after hanging out at his apartment. While I was unloading the dishwasher, there was a sudden thunderstorm and I shrieked after hearing a crazy-loud crack of thunder. I recall thinking about calling my dad, but I didn't.

The next day, on May 2, a Friday, I went to school as on any other day, with after-school plans to play in an out-of-town high school softball game. The game took place during an absolutely perfect crystal-clear spring day on a pristine field. I pitched a no-hitter—a highlight of my softball career. The bus got us back to my school around 5:30 or 6 p.m. and I called my mother to come pick me up. I was surprised when my neighbor answered the phone and told me my mother was busy. Betty said, "*I'm* going to come get you."

In the 15 minutes before Betty arrived to retrieve me, I went to get a Pepsi from the vending machine because throwing a no-hitter can make you parched! I was trying to put together change for a can and the machine randomly started spewing out cans of all kinds of soda. It seemed like dozens! Other teammates were grabbing whatever was coming out of the mouth of the machine. I grabbed two cans, drank one right down and, when Betty picked me up, I took the other one home tucked safely in my glove.

Betty and I were riding on Route 9, and I remember it being an awkward, small talk-filled car ride. Betty was probably nervous thinking about the news I was about to hear.

As we crossed over Grayson's Pond bridge, I saw a snippet of a perfect rainbow; it had no beginning and no end, just a colored patch of light. I learned, much later in life, it's called a sundog. I had never consciously remembered seeing a rainbow like this before. I was obsessed with weather growing up, so I probably would have noticed. In fact, I would sleep with the window open in the winter just to watch for meteor showers and any other meteorological highlight that occurred. The majority of my child-hood I believed I would be a weather forecaster or meteorologist when I grew up. Years later, when I came out in 2000, I took the sundog viewing rainbow on that day as a sign from my dad that he would have accepted me being gay.

Betty brought me home and walked inside with me. We walked into a chaotic kitchen scene. I saw my mom, but then I also saw two of her closest family members. "What the heck is going on?" I wondered as I made my way into the room.

Everyone was buzzing around. I have no recollection of where Amanda was. My mom was sitting in a kitchen chair and saw me when I walked in the side door. My family looked at me with an odd sadness that perplexed me. "What's going on?" I asked my mother as she invited me to come sit on her lap (an uncommon occurrence especially at 15). Brushing the knots out of my tangled hair with her fingers, she looked me in the eye and directly, no flowery language, said quietly, "Daddy died of a heart attack today."

I went into hysterics. My mother, tears falling from already red eyes down her puffy cheeks, pulled me to her chest, rocked with me for a little while, and we sat crying together. When we pulled apart, she looked at me and I got up and left the room. I couldn't take the oppressive feeling of the house.

I went outside and sat next to a tree stump with my cat, sobbing, alone for the remainder of the night.

That second can of Pepsi, which I had brought home with me that day, convinced it was a gift sent by my dad, sat on the desk in my bedroom for several years until one day, there was a pinhole leak and the soda seeped out. So, then I had an empty Pepsi can that continued to sit on my desk. Later, when our house burned down, that can became scorched and squished in all the fire activity. I still kept the crushed can of Pepsi for a long time. I felt it was some kind of sign from my dad that he knew I was thirsty and he wanted to treat all my friends and teammates. He was letting me know he was thinking of me as he passed from this world to beyond.

A while after my dad had passed away, I was asked to pick what I wanted to keep from the house before the junk was going to be cleared out. I selected some ham radio equipment my dad had used for sending and receiving Morse code. These machines, like the Pepsi can, found a home on my desk shelf.

More signs from my father came when, out of nowhere, more than once, this equipment would randomly start tapping out Morse code. It would freak me out, seriously. Was my dad trying to talk with me? I didn't have the mental capacity in the moment to recognize what was happening and translate the code. I still don't know what it said. I had the machines until the fire destroyed them.

My parents were not yet legally divorced when he died, but my father had a girlfriend, Rhonda. She was a short, rotund woman with a flair for the dramatic and had been a longtime friend of both my parents. When I was younger, I played with Rhonda's daughter Leah sometimes, so our family knew their family. In the months leading up to my father's death, my mom and Rhonda hated each other—which appeared to have stemmed from their fighting for my dad. I didn't like Rhonda on principle, simply because my mom hated her.

Rhonda couldn't reach my father to arrange their weekend plans and had decided to go to my dad's apartment. When she went to his temporary below-grade basement apartment that Friday morning, saw his Jeep in the driveway, and couldn't get in, worried, she called the police. That's how we found out he had died. My guess is that Rhonda was still at the apartment when the squad car arrived.

My mom was insecure and probably jealous of Rhonda, so after everyone made a fuss about poor Rhonda finding her boyfriend dead, how horrible that must be for her, and so on … with hatred and venom in her voice mom would rant about Rhonda inappropriately acting like "the grieving widow."

My father passed on a Friday. The wake was held on Monday, and Tuesday was the funeral. I was a mess, so the details are somewhat blurry about what transpired all weekend, but certain things stood out.

My father's apartment, located on a side street, was dark and dank. It was not disgusting—it was oddly clean, but really gloomy because it was below ground and the windows were small and weren't located with natural light in mind. Unlike the clutter in our yard at the house, his apartment was very well organized—I didn't mind spending time there.

Barbara, my dad's sister, and her son showed up from out of state and wanted to go into my dad's apartment, I didn't know what was happening. I think Barbara told my mother she wanted to stay there while in town. As soon as Barbara got the keys to my dad's place, she started loading up her van full of my dad's stuff without asking anybody. I don't know how this was legal? I remember Barbara filling boxes and cartons with his stuff. She took his clothes, electronics, and most of his guns. It all happened really, really fast.

At some point, when Rhonda saw Barbara taking things, Rhonda made some comment about a big fish tank and how she and my dad had bought the tank together and so on. I knew that he had picked that tank up on the side of the road somewhere because I was with him. That is the story that threw me over the edge. Add to the mix of yelling one hysterical 15-year-old to whom no one was paying attention. I realized that these adults were all making stuff up and taking things and my dad was gone. My mother, Amanda, and I were too distraught to protect ourselves from these people or think of things we would want to keep. There was a wake and a funeral to get through.

At the end of the day, after burying my dad and all the relatives snagging things while I was kind of out of it and numb, I remember I was able to grab a couple of sweatshirts that were my dad's. They had his smell. My uncle, to this day, has some of my dad's shotguns in storage for me. And, eventually, I inherited my dad's 1993 red Jeep Wrangler a month before I turned 16. Luckily for me, because my parents were not yet legally divorced, the ownership of his Jeep was not in question.

But honestly, everything moved so fast, everything disappeared so quickly, and we were left with almost zero. If losing a parent isn't difficult enough, adding the drama and antics of squabbling adults makes it exponentially harder.

PART III

DNA

Ages: 16-19

June 1997-February 2000

Age 16

Because my dad was super-handy and always fixing things, we had a computer in our house way before other people did. I had my very own old DOS computer in my room when I was still in middle school. I remember doing basic C++ coding on it to create smiley faces and animations. I locked myself in my room when I wasn't working one of my winter part-time jobs to keep me away from Amanda. I had to distract myself with something. I didn't know how to exist without being in motion or doing something. And along came the Internet to keep me fully engaged!

My mother was clueless about technology. I could have been doing anything up in my room (and I was) and she wouldn't know and wouldn't try to figure it out. This is likely why this misbehavior started after my dad passed as he 100% would have known how to trace my Internet steps.

Earlier that year, I got my first job at a local family-owned ice cream shop. With the continued strong urge to be out of my house, as soon as I was able to get a job, I did. Working in an ice cream shop for one summer can impact how you feel about the sugary treat for the rest of your life. I certainly took advantage of my access to free ice cream and overloaded. But the best part of the job was working with my two friends Samantha and Emily. Emily and I had played softball together for years and were on the same school bus, but we hadn't been close. Once I got the job there, I met Samantha and the three of us became inseparable.

This whole cyber adventure started in 1997. Because I was the only one with a computer, my friends all came to my house, my bedroom, to do whatever we wanted to do. Clicking away on the keyboard, we would find unsuspecting guys and prey on them. We assumed these guys were in their twenties. They would send us "dick pics"—before this was a common Internet and mobile device occurrence. I thought it was disgusting, but I played along.

Part III: DNA

One of us, usually Emily, was operating the computer and the rest of us were chiming in with directions, advice, and comments. I was 16 and Samantha and Emily were 17.

When it got dark, we would get revenge on these guys who sent offensive pictures by pretending to give the men directions to my house—but instead send them on a wild-goose chase with directions taking them into large loops. We wasted their time. We were cock teasers.

By the time they got back to their computer they would send us hateful, vile emails or message us in the chat rooms. Of course, we would never give them a home phone number (this was pre-cell phones).

We would laugh and get some kind of high from this, feeling a sense of empowerment and victory over these men.

At the time, I still didn't realize I was gay. I didn't realize that how I felt toward Samantha, in particular, was anything other than friendship. Just wanting to brush the hair out of her eyes or hold her hand while we were walking seemed to be something friends did. I had slept over at girls' houses and other girls seemed to play with hair and sit close, giggle, laugh, and stuff like that. "It's what girls do," I thought. Thinking of all of my close friends, Samantha was the only one who caused me to have butterflies in my stomach when I was around her. When I knew I was seeing her or working with her, I would be excited. I wanted to breathe the air she breathed and would have done anything she asked of me. I would have physically hurt anyone who caused Samantha any pain at all. So, when we started to flirt with guys in cyber chat rooms, I was little protective, a lot defensive, and I moved into what could only be called mother hen behavior.

I was staring at my love across my bedroom, illuminated by the computer monitor, and I did not know I loved her. Unrequited love is where love songs, poems, and artwork come from. I don't think the girls knew how I felt, because I'm not sure I fully understood what I was feeling. You don't

43

know what you don't know, until you have a light-bulb moment—that flash of insight. My flash had yet to come.

We found ourselves in many dangerous situations as a result of our frequenting AOL chat rooms. We'd be running from people, driving 80 or 90 mph on the highway, fearing for our lives, because my friends really pissed off some guys. I would protect my friends with my life, or apparently, with my car. Sometimes it felt like we'd robbed a bank and were in the getaway car. I was a nervous wreck, praying we wouldn't wreck the car, but my BFFs were getting stimulated by the danger. And things just kept getting more and more out of control. Like with drugs or alcohol, tolerance builds up and you have to keep pushing further, doing more to get the same high.

Age 17

I was graduating high school and about to turn 18 when I started Chicks with Sticks. This idea came after Emily and I made an effort to not be embarrassed for my backyard high school graduation party. Emily and I got to work on my yard one spring afternoon after school. We had music blasting from the deck. We put out some snacks and beverages. We paid my sister to go away and leave us alone. And we danced and worked around the yard making the place suitable to invite all our friends over. We had so much fun doing it, when we finished up, we cleaned Emily's yard too. When we finished both yards, floating around in my tattered aboveground pool with Samantha, we had a brainstorm. I blurted out, "Why don't we start a landscaping business?" We figured why not get paid for having so much fun? *Brilliant*, we decided.

And, though not having any idea at all about what we were doing, we went ahead and started a landscaping company. We went door to door offering our services. We worked on some neighbors' lawns and made some money. We pulled plants and weeds, cleaned up yards, cut lawns, and planted things for people. Whatever they needed. Nothing too complicated. So what, if we accidentally cut out someone's rose bushes? We were young and inexpensive to hire and there was a market for that. We made a little money and got ambitious. We wanted *more* money.

So, we picked a name, Chicks with Sticks (clever, right?), and ran one ad—just once—in a local weekly paper called *The Notice* and waited to see what happened. We got two calls. One was from a landscape company looking to hire help. Not what we were hoping for. The second call for Chicks with Sticks was from a woman named Maria, who lived in the town next to us, about 25 minutes away—a more promising lead.

The advertisement had included Emily's home phone number so, naturally, Emily answered the calls. I sat next to Emily and fed her answers to our potential customer's questions. When Maria called, after a few minutes of Emily talking to her, Maria became irritated as Emily was turning and asking me every question she was being asked. Maria said, "Let me talk to whoever you're talking to! This is ridiculous!" So, I got on the phone and made arrangements for Emily and me to go by and look at Maria's yard to give her an estimate.

On a sunny Saturday in June we walked up to Maria's front door. We knocked. We waited. It seemed that people were home—there were cars in the driveway, the front door was open, and music was playing in the house— but no one came to the door, even when we called out. Being young and impatient, we said, "To heck with it for now, we'll call her later."

When we called later, no one answered the phone. That was just weird. After a few weeks of nothing happening, Emily and I felt defeated and gave up landscaping, figuring that if they're all like this, why bother? We had short teenage attention spans and were already moving on to our next big adventure.

Age 18

At the same time Emily and I were dabbling in landscaping and I was graduating from high school, I had also begun the search for my birth mother.

I had always known that as soon as I was 18, I would start my quest. I never felt like I fit in anywhere. I hoped that finding my birth family would fill the void and give me answers.

Despite all our mutual baggage, I did love my mother and I didn't want to upset her. I was super-cautious that anything I did could send my mother into a drunken rage or depression. One time when I had asked, she grinned and said, "What? Do you want to leave me now?" I know she was kidding, but still, there is truth in everything. I don't think she realized how serious I was about finding answers.

Many times, I simply didn't feel like a whole person. I felt that I needed to know where I came from, who I take after. I wanted to know if my birth mother was still alive or dead. If she was living close by or somewhere else. Moreover, if she thought about me. To a certain degree, of course, I knew myself, but at the same time, I knew absolutely nothing. Never being able to answer a medical questionnaire or have any idea what illnesses I was susceptible to were common worries of mine.

Instead of pushing my mother for answers, I poked around. I looked through her things to find papers. I found nothing on my adoption, but plenty on Amanda. That seemed odd to me.

Next, I looked on the Internet, doing some research to see what I could find out on my own. In 1999, finding a birth parent was a much more arduous process than it is now—and, even today, it is still very challenging for many. After a bit of Internet searching, I was stunned by the volume of data I would have to go through to find my birth mother.

Instead of overwhelming myself further, I reached out to my Aunt Debbie (my mother's sister-in-law), who had always been my closest aunt. I always felt like she, too, was an odd duck in our family and, as a result, we were close.

I explained to Debbie via email why I didn't want to go to my mother. I outlined for my aunt everything I had tried already to find my birth parents' information. "I am specifically focused on my birth mother," I shared. (My birth father never held as much significance.) I wrote to

Debbie about how I rifled through folders in the house—I had found nothing, not one kind of adoption paper or anything. I had rummaged through a filing cabinet and I had asked my mother directly and got only limited answers. I assumed my mother knew more than she really did. In the end, it appeared that, for the most part, my mom was honest about the limited information she knew.

I finished my email with a plea:

> *… Do you know any information at all??? I know she talks to you the most out of all the family and I thought maybe she talked to you about this.*

The tone of my email was much more direct than usual (our email banter was usually sarcastic and playful), but this time I meant business.

Shockingly, Debbie responded quickly and briefly:

> *I want you to come over to my house as soon as you can. I have something here that will help you. I have had it for five years and have been waiting for this day. I was going to keep it forever. If you never asked, I was never going to show it to you. Come over soon, we have a lot to talk about. And thank you for this. I am honored that you asked me.*
> *Love,*
> *Aunt Debbie*

Nervous. Excited. Terrified. A few days later, I told my mother a believable white lie—that I was going to Aunt Debbie's to help her fix her computer—and I headed over to see this mysterious "something."

When I arrived, Debbie and I went out onto her back deck. But before she would show me the "something," she grilled me—she was protecting me, she said. She peppered me with a litany of questions and warnings, from the benign, "Do I know what I'm doing?" to the ludicrous, "She could be a toothless hooker."

She made it clear that once I opened Pandora's box, I couldn't change my mind and shut it. Exasperated and frustrated, I blurted out, "I just want to ask my birth mother some questions!" Finally, with trepidation, she handed me a newspaper clipping to read. I didn't know what I was looking at. It was a short article in the "Afternoon Tea" section of the *Princeton Gazette*, where local aspiring writers could submit their works. After all the suspense around it had given it such a charge, I couldn't immediately grasp what exactly I was reading, so I had to reread it, paying closer attention.

I knew my name had been Katie and that I was born with red hair. I gripped the newspaper article, held it in the air at Debbie, and shrieked, "Oh, my God!" Aunt Debbie nodded, tossed me a knowing look and said, "I think you're ready for me to tell you the whole story …"

In 1994, when I was 13, Aunt Debbie was reading the "Afternoon Tea" section of the *Princeton Gazette*, which was her weekend routine. This particular day she stumbled across an essay titled "*I Gave My Baby to Adoring Parents.*"

The headline had caught her attention and, as the details in the article began to unfold, it slowly confirmed her belief that this article was written about me by my birth mother. Key information that sealed the deal in my aunt's mind was that I was given to a Catholic adoption agency, note of my red hair and blue eyes, the timing of the article, and dating my birth to 1981. The clincher was that the essay ended with "for Katie"—my given name at birth.

My aunt agonized over what to do with this article and whom to tell. She ultimately opted to tuck it into her wallet for when the time was right—five years later to be exact—when I showed up on her back deck.

"So, what will you do now?" Aunt Debbie asked me.

Still spinning from the whole story, I shrugged and said, "I have to find the author of this article, of course."

I left my aunt's and went straight to Emily's house with the frayed article in my hand. Part of this was easy, as there was both a photo of the woman and her name printed right at the top of the page. The newspaper was local. But was the woman a local person or had she moved? The most basic thing was to check the phone book, right? So, Emily got out her phone book. And we sat there staring at the book on the table.

Emily was growing impatient with me. Hours passed before I felt emotionally ready to look the woman up. All the horror stories I had heard about people searching for their birth families for decades, and all I had to do was look in the phone book. It seemed too easy. Nothing in my life had been easy—so I assumed this, too, wouldn't be.

The last name of the author of the article was Tiller. My eyes quickly scanned the page of Tillers. I stopped when I saw the address on Capen Drive. Something about that address sounded familiar. My computer brain was processing, and I suddenly put the connection together and screamed. Emily jumped.

"WHAT?"

"Hello?" I said. I was shaking Emily, I wanted her to figure it out too. "Maria? At 68 Capen Drive? Isn't that the address where no one answered our knock a month ago?" Emily didn't get it yet. "… for our landscaping estimate!?" I continued.

And then Emily got it. Her eyes opened wide, she grabbed the article, and looked back at me.

The article was written by Maria Tiller. The same name as the woman who needed yard work for a party a month prior. What were the chances that the woman who wanted Chicks with Sticks to do landscaping was my birth mother?

I nervously dialed her number.

Fortunately, or because of fate, Maria answered the phone and stated that it was just her bad luck that the landscaper she hired never showed up, and her party was only three days away. She asked if we could come by her house the next morning to provide an estimate. I was supposed to be taking care of Amanda the next day, but I figured I could get out of it. I told Maria we could be there in the morning.

We talked a little more before hanging up. I was purposely providing clues about myself to see if Maria would react. Was she looking for her daughter?

Because of the closed adoption, both of us had basic non-identifying information. I knew my birth mother was one of six kids. My birth mother knew I was adopted by a nurse and an electrician and that my dad had sisters and my mom had brothers.

I told Maria how Emily and I have been really busy cleaning our own yards, because we had graduation parties, and that I also just had a birthday. Maria asked when my birthday was, "In case we fall and crack our heads open while landscaping her property," she said. I told her I'd just turned 18 and provided my exact birthday. We hung up the phone. Would she get curious by my birthdate? My age? I spent all evening wondering and questioning. I could not sleep.

As Emily and I approached the house, we could see Maria standing at the window, watching us walk up to the door. She greeted us outside, carrying pitchers of water, some cups, and a radio. She was assessing me, and I was assessing her.

We walked casually around the yard while she was giving us directions, "Rake this over here, pull this out over here, tidy up this area," and so on. We gave Maria a price and she hired us to do the work. We would start immediately. Maria headed off to her job at a carpeting company.

Later that afternoon, Emily and I were talking during a beverage break and Emily made a comment that stamped itself permanently on my brain. She said, "Just think, we could be sitting in your birth mother's back yard." What a wild thought!

The following afternoon at five, Emily and I were supposed to go back to Maria's to be paid. At this point, getting paid was the last thing on my mind. I had been stressing the entire night before and couldn't stop thinking about how I would handle our encounter when Maria got home at five o'clock.

I had the presence of mind to bring along my birth certificate, a photocopy of the article in which I highlighted in orange marker the areas that were directly relevant to me, and a baby picture. I was determined to have confirmation, one way or another.

We arrived at Maria's along with Samantha, who didn't want to miss this moment. When we arrived, Maria had a pool full of children playing out in the back. When she saw Emily and me approaching, she got up and went into the house, presumably to get our check. I thought we did a good job, but Maria said nothing. She was acting casual and nonchalant—borderline aloof.

If she was who I thought she was, I would have thought her heart would have been jumping out of her chest like mine was! Instead of getting paid or talking about what I wanted to talk about, I found myself being introduced to a pet turtle who lived in an aquarium near the door. I kept thinking, "I need to say something. Say something! *Anything*!" And yet I was standing around making small talk with everyone and I just didn't know how to ask the question I had in my heart and head for almost 18 years!

Maria handed us an envelope, said goodbye, and then suddenly, like an afterthought, asked if we could come back the next week to mulch. What? A little confused, I immediately said, "Yes."

I forced myself to hang back as I shooed Emily out the front door. I summoned every ounce of courage an 18-year-old can muster and said, "Can I speak to you privately?"

She led me out the side door, where we stood together near a porch swing but had a view of the kids in the pool.

"Um, do you like to write?" I opened with.

"Yes, I do," said Maria.

I removed the folded copy of the article out of my back pocket and hesitantly asked, squinting at her in the sun, "Are you the same Maria who wrote this?" and handed her the paper.

"Yes. Why?" she asked.

"Did you find your daughter yet?" I queried.

"No, she's not old enough," she responded.

My heart immediately sank and I began to panic. Did I get the dates wrong and miscalculate the year of her daughter's birth? Was all this for nothing? Maria had to have seen the sheer panic in my eyes because she immediately followed up with, "State law says she has to be 21."

Wasting no time, I blurted, "I think this article is about me."

"Are you adopted?" she asked.

"Yes." I said.

"What hospital were you born in?"

"Walden County."

"Is your mother a nurse?" she said, sounding more excited.

"Yes."

"Is your father an electrician?"

"Yes."

"Does your mother only have brothers?"

"Yes."

"Does your father only have sisters?"

"Yes."

"I brought my birth certificate and a baby picture," I added as I handed them to her.

The picture was from the hospital, the day I was born.

Maria quickly stated, "Come into the house."

Maria turned to an organizer on her counter and started flipping through, searching for something. She didn't seem to be able to find it and said, "I have to show you something, but I can't find it. Give me a moment."

I went into the front yard to tell my friends what was happening. I told them, "I think it's her! She said she has something to show me. I've gotta go back in. Can you go for a drive and come back in a bit?" I asked them hopefully. Of course, they said no problem and took off.

When I got back into the house, Maria had unearthed a file and said, "My proof. Eighteen years of letters and little poems." But the kicker was that she pulled out the very same hospital photo that I was holding. It was like finding the yin to the yang.

Three or four times during the course of the evening, Emily and Samantha drove by, only to be waved away. Finally, at about 10:30 p.m., Maria invited them to come in and join us. They were so excited for me. We ended up there until past midnight.

We chatted, sometimes all at the same time, exclaiming over all the common ground between my birth mother and me:

- We both hate mayonnaise.
- For a few years, we both attended the same church where I went to elementary school. We figured we must have encountered each other there at some point.
- I also learned that when Maria was pregnant with me, she could not walk down the tomato sauce aisle of the supermarket without feeling nauseated. We found this funny because I hated tomato sauce, even on pizza.

The children Maria was watching in the pool were my brother (nine years my junior) and his two friends. It was one of their birthdays. She took a knife to her friend's son's birthday cake and said, "I've never given you cake in your life. Here's your first piece of cake from me."

When we finally said goodbye late that night, we both stood in the doorway for a long time. And then Maria said what I was thinking, "We should have a hug, huh?"

We did.

It was a long, warm, satisfying hug that made us both want to cry. It felt completely natural to me and then Maria said, as if reading my mind, "It feels like we've been hugging all our lives, doesn't it?" And I hugged her again as I nodded my head into her chest.

Over the next few days, Maria and I were so ecstatic about getting to know each other, we would be in hyperdrive with questions and stories and sharing photos. And then we'd find ourselves completely enervated and, just when we'd downshift, we'd suddenly burst into overtired laughing. We couldn't stop talking to each other—trying to make up for the last 18 years!

Maria admitted to me one day that she had always been afraid that her kid would find her and then say, "How nice to meet you. I hate your guts." That thought never had crossed my mind. I eased her mind by responding with "That's ridiculous, Maria. In fact, I admire you for having given me up. You did it for me. I get that."

To this point, it had all been too easy. Now the hard part came—I had to tell my mother.

I was so afraid to even bring up the subject because this had all transpired behind my mom's back so quickly. The whole search from start to finish was less than two weeks. Would she have a total meltdown? Would she kick me out? Would she feel betrayed and take it out on me? Would she drink herself into a stupor? I didn't know how to approach this safely.

So again, I turned to my Aunt Debbie for advice. She offered to come over to the house so we could break the news to my mother together. That was a huge relief. I had a partner in crime, so to speak.

My mom knew something was up. She was looking at me suspiciously and asked, "What are you two up to now?" My Aunt Debbie and I were known tricksters when together.

We all went out to the back deck and I started telling my mother the story. She broke down in tears and I got choked up, so my aunt did the rest of the talking. My mom immediately said she thought she and Maria should meet.

They waited about a month to get acclimated to the new situation and then made a date to meet at a local restaurant near where Maria lived.

My mom was in a state over it. "I'm meeting some woman. A stranger. What is she going to think?" she kept asking me.

Maria also admitted that she was "coming unglued." As the two of them separately related their encounter to me I learned that, when my mom arrived, they immediately connected and hugged. My mom's first words were, "Thank you for giving me her." They spent three hours together, in what would turn out to be the longest conversation in their entire relationship.

Months later, my mother mentioned that she'd noticed Maria and I had the same hands. Another time, she said that Maria and I had the same texture hair. My mother kept noticing things that Maria and I had in common every time she mentally replayed their one three-hour encounter.

More than five months after the seismic reunification event, my mom was still coping with the new information. She admitted to feeling a little jealousy, a sense of having lost her "little girl."

She had always thought she'd be the one to help me find my birth mother. "And all of a sudden, after 18 years of waiting for you to ask me, to find out—bing, bang, boom—you've gone on your own and found her." She was admittedly hurt.

From this point onward, I straddled two worlds—two families. The next encounter between my birth mother and (adoptive) mother wouldn't be for another 12 years when they were both walking me down the aisle at my wedding.

As my eighteenth summer ended, I started classes at the local community college and would randomly stop by Maria's house between classes or I'd go after classes and we'd stay up late talking. Soon after starting community college, I realized I didn't actually hate school as much as I had believed up to this point. Excitedly, I began visiting four-year colleges throughout New England. I was starting to see a way out—light at the end of the tunnel.

When I first met Maria, holidays would come and I'd want to spend them with her, but also wanted to be with my family. So, no matter where I was, I felt I like I shouldn't be there. Everyone has routines of things they do around the holidays, and here I was at 18, suddenly thrown into a whole new family and all of their festivities and traditions. It just felt weird, like I didn't belong, even though I was never intentionally treated like I didn't belong.

Feeling like an outsider was all in my own head. I dreamt that when I found my birth parents, the whole family would have red hair and freckles. If everyone had red hair, would I have felt like I belonged? My birth grandmother and aunt both dyed their hair red. Should that have helped me connect? Looking like someone had been my longtime vision of what family would look like. I finally decided it must be something bigger or deeper than matching freckles to connect family.

When I met my brother Ryan for the first time, he was nine. When people saw us together, they could see we were related and yet we didn't have similar coloring. Since my only interaction with younger kids had been with my sister,

Amanda, and I really disliked her (I didn't like children in general), I didn't know how to act around Ryan. I didn't know how to communicate with him—and in many ways, I still don't. When Amanda came into my life, I was entering elementary school and she was just a toddler. When I'd met Ryan, I was heading off to college and he had not even gone through puberty. It has always felt like I was out of sync with creating familial relationships all around.

The only time Ryan and I totally connected was in more recent years. I went to Northern California in 2015 for a speaking engagement and he worked in Silicon Valley. Ryan gave me a tour of the corporate campus where he worked. We sat around for a few hours and then he took me out in his prized Porsche for a bit of sightseeing. It was the first time we spent time alone together away from other family. It was a good experience. We were able to have an adult discussion about business and work and relate on that safe "professional" level.

I had been out shopping for the day. My friends, Stacy and Samantha, were with me in Walden, randomly looking for white sneaker cleaner at a local pharmacy. A normal, unremarkable kind of late fall day. The sun was out and made the day feel warmer than the temperature would indicate. Christmas was coming and the stores and streets were decorated festively. I was looking forward to winter break from my first semester of college. All was good in the world until Emily paged Samantha with a "911" message.

Samantha called back from a payphone outside and heard that Emily was listening to reports on the police scanner that announced my home was on fire! The three of us panicked and immediately ran for the car. Samantha went into movie hero action mode driving the car and Stacy, with two older brothers who were volunteer firemen, was trying to calm me down and tell me everything was going to be fine with all the authority that an insider-view of emergency responders could command.

Samantha drove me home doing 100 miles per hour on the 11 miles of highway between Walden and Concord. The car ride was a complete blur. What would have normally been a 20- to 25-minute ride felt like we got there in 10 minutes. Samantha had NASCAR-level driving skills that had come in handy for getting us out of dangerous situations many times, and this time it got us safely to my home as it was burning to the ground.

When we got to my street, we couldn't get through. It was blocked off by fire trucks and police personnel trying to keep the area safe. At first, I couldn't understand what I was seeing: Why was there a giant swimming pool set up at the top of our road and how on earth did the hoses to that pool extend to my house a quarter mile from there? I learned that our road did not have access to fire hydrants and that if the firemen needed water, they needed to hose it in from the main street. (Ultimately, I believe the damage to my home may have been less if we had adequate access to fire hydrants in our town. But we didn't, so the responders had to wait for the trucked-in water to put out the blaze.) I don't know when I learned of this, but I suspect Stacy may have been trying to explain these things as I was frantically screaming that I needed to get by. I'm certain I wasn't coherent at this time, as I had already been in hysterics over the thought of a fire, not knowing how bad it was.

When I explained to the emergency personnel that it was my house and my family, they let me pass on foot. I sprinted down the road to our house and, as I rounded the corner, I had a full view of how bad the fire really was. I was surrounded by flashing lights, fire trucks, firemen everywhere, water shooting from hoses, smoke and flames billowing out from open windows … it was a full 4-alarm fire. At the time, I didn't know what a 4-alarm fire meant. I didn't know the difference in those terms between a simple grease fire contained to a kitchen with one fire truck responding, versus a full-blown house fire with many fire trucks trying to contain an unwieldy blaze.

I was just one hysterical teenager in a hoodie added to the conglomeration of strangers and neighbors standing at the end of my driveway, until I realized I couldn't locate my family and my mind went straight to panic mode—thinking my sister and mother and all our pets were still inside the flaming house.

Before I could ask anyone about my family, I heard my name. I couldn't attach the male voice to a body … just a disembodied, "Jenn!" hanging in the air. Our adjacent neighbor finally reached me and assured me that my mother and sister were fine and at my next-door neighbor's house. A wave of relief hit me like an anvil on my chest, but not a heavy enough weight to stop me from sprinting across the lawn to find my family. After hearing that, the time it took me to get to the neighbor's doorstep felt like Olympic-level track speed. I didn't know what I would be walking into.

I ran without waiting for Samantha and Stacy. Samantha was hooked on crime and justice and things in this realm, so she relished standing outside watching the action as the fire was put out. Stacy grew up with brothers who were firemen, so this didn't impact her in any negative way. My two best friends stood outside and watched everything disintegrate as I walked into the chaos of my neighbor's home.

If my life were a movie, from the moment of the first text that seemed to slow time into stilted, distorted minutes, to the high-speed race to get to my family, to the slow silenced moments of recognition and overwhelm where only my heartbeat could be heard in my head, my life was alternating between super-fast speed to slow motion. Recollections of what transpired would arrive back into my mind slowly over the next days, weeks, and years.

When I walked into the neighbor's Cape-style house, there was more commotion. Not only were my mother and sister in my neighbor's front living room, but also the neighbors, and a bevy of fire and police personnel. I don't know how long my family had been sitting there, but long enough to be wrapped in blankets and drinking hot cocoa.

I immediately collapsed on my mother's lap in a very similar fashion to the day she told me my dad had died. We both sobbed on the couch for a few minutes as Amanda was wrapped under my mom's free arm. It didn't take long until my mind went to worrying about the cats. I don't know who urged, perhaps forced, me to remain in the neighbor's house, but I obeyed despite my adrenaline pushing me to flee. I eventually went outside to see that the fire had been put out and cried out as the entire left side of the house was unrecognizable; the side of the house where my bedroom was.

From the outside, it was clear that a fire had ravaged the house, but it looked isolated to just the left side. The right two-thirds of the house didn't seem nearly as bad—from the outside, anyway. I went into search-and-rescue mode for my cats.

Firemen and police personnel were still milling about, undoubtedly looking for the cause of the fire. While I don't recall now that my mom ever took showers at night, I had heard her tell a police officer that she was in the shower when the fire started. It struck me as odd at the time for her to be showering at 8 p.m., but I didn't give it another thought as finding the cats was my priority.

As I walked through the soggy ground, kicking debris and feeling flakes of singed objects floating about and settling on my clothing, I frantically called my cats' names. At the time, we had four, as we often did, but my priority was finding my two-year-old cat Pumpkin. I searched for hours, calling her name until my throat was sore, but I never found her nor her remains.

My mother convincingly told me about Amanda playing with a candle, and I threw a hateful look toward my little sister. I didn't trust her after everything she had done to disrupt and disturb my room, my possessions, and my life. My mother's retelling of the story was that Amanda had been trying to light a candle and accidentally dropped it on the recliner, which caught fire. Once that recliner caught, the other one did, then the bookcase, and so on. I am not sure what she actually intended to do with that candle—or if a candle was ever really involved.

After the fire, for a few days, my sister, mother, and I stayed with my mom's brother. My patience for close quarters with so much family didn't work for me, so I opted to rotate time between Maria's and Samantha's homes. It was easy packing each time I moved again because nearly everything I owned fit into a laundry basket that I toted from home to home. After playing musical couches for a few days, I decided it would be easier to just stay with Maria for a few weeks. It seemed like the logical thing to do, especially since I was there so much before and after school and work anyway.

I lived with my birth mother for two weeks but surprised myself when I decided I wanted to be with my family. For all my complaining about everything at home, I missed them. I packed up my basket and went to live with my mother and sister in the mobile home they had set up on our property where we were planning to rebuild. We had a few happy moments as we decorated for Christmas and tried to make the best of our temporary home.

It seemed—as anyone will tell you who has gone through this—very surreal. It's like you're watching a movie about yourself, starring you, but you're not really feeling anything in the moment. The pain comes later. When the loss hits you. When you think about how you can't wait to go home and curl up in bed because you're so exhausted, but then you remember you don't have a home or a bed. It was a horrible day. And it was just the beginning of a period of long days and nights.

PART IV

DESIRE

Ages: 19-25

November 2000-May 2007

Age 19

After completing one semester at community college, I passed on applying to transfer to a four-year college and instead took on a full-time job. I wasn't sure what my path forward would look like, but I knew I was able to take some control back through work. I found that I could push my body and mind, forget about all the personal bullshit, and excel at something. I would demonstrate to myself and others that I could be successful at something other than softball.

I got my first full-time job in a factory that made parts for refrigerators. I had been working since I was able at age 16—multiple jobs, usually, but this was the first time I was working a full 40-hour work week, earning an hourly wage plus overtime with benefits from a single employer.

My pay was $9.10 an hour. This included an extra $1.00 an hour because I worked second shift, 3 p.m. to 11 p.m. I liked pushing my body. Many months passed working at this job. It wasn't rewarding in any way, but I was making $3 more an hour than minimum wage and it felt amazing to be making so much more than my friends.

In this factory, I started off in the packing area (because that's where women worked) to box and ship the parts. The place was mostly men. At about 19 years old, the men thought of me like their daughter. I felt safe working there.

I've always been frustrated by inefficiencies; it's just something that drives me crazy. If I see that there's a faster, better, more effective way of doing something, I'm going to fix it. If there was an effective shortcut, why wouldn't you take that shortcut and be more efficient?

At the plant, I managed to subtly change the way the packing department was laid out. I noticed that the way the parts came off the line was adding an extra unnecessary step. On an assembly line, every second counts. They let me help redesign the system and that helped persuade them that I could be helpful in other areas of the line as well. I worked my way through the entire assembly line hitting every single area except for painting, which required a specialized license.

Once I started moving around the factory floor, I was no longer bored because I was learning from one job to the next, moseying my way through the whole process. I adapted to being in an environment where you're one of four women out of hundreds of men and you're immediately classified based on assumptions like, "She couldn't possibly do this." I had to prove myself. And prove myself I did.

As a female, gaining credibility from the guys is harder and it takes a lot longer. It's almost an accomplishment and a hurdle at the same time. I thought, "Well, the hell with this, I'm just going to do it my way." And there I was, eventually ending up in the welding area of the line, with no formal training. The guy I ended up welding with was a really tall (6'4") Kenyan man. He and I worked side by side with me standing at just shy of 5'3". We looked like quite the unconventional pairing.

I made friends with everybody. It worked out well and I enjoyed it a lot. It was the most physically intense and grueling job, but it's one of my fonder work experiences when I look back. This job gives me immense perspective, even today, about what a hard day of work feels like. No matter how bad a day I might be having, I think back to the fact that I could have singed arm hair off at work, and all feels better. Also, I have a fun party trick I bust out from time to time—I can essentially handle extremely hot cups, plates, you name it—as a result of really screwing up the sensitivity in my hands from improperly handling scalding hot metal. There's always a bright side, right? Who needs potholders?

During this time, I was living at Samantha's, but I wasn't home all that much and when I was, I was sleeping. Working 3 p.m. to 11 p.m. was an interesting experience. I would be up until about 3 a.m. or 4 a.m. every morning because I needed time to unwind before I went to bed. Most nights, I ended up hanging out at my friend Stacy's house, where she would cook us dinner at 11:15 p.m. when I got out of work.

Six months after they tore down what remained of my home, I was at the factory and I met a woman whose house had burned down 25 years before. When we first began speaking about it, I couldn't wrap my head around how the fire had impacted her 25 years later. She told me that it is an experience you can never shake; that it will follow you forever. "It is like a death of a human," she shared, "where traces of your past creep in and the realization of all that you've lost hits you like a wave of grief, like it happened just yesterday." Her words have stuck with me even as I passed the 20-year anniversary of my house fire. She was absolutely right—it's an experience you just don't shake. It changes you forever. I often find myself saying to my son, "You know … that [enter any item here] is 21 years old." And it occurred to me recently that he'll never hear me reference anything from my childhood because that part of my life was snuffed out.

Samantha convinced me that I should call out of work to go on a double date. We didn't usually double date, as I was never interested. I had been dating a guy for a while who I had broken up with earlier in the year. She had been dating Brian, a chef at the chain hotel where she worked as a housekeeper. Brian had a good friend in town from Zurich, Switzerland.

It was a classic New England fall day when I set out to find a date-night outfit. Samantha drove us to Walden Place (a local mall) where she practically pushed me into the Express store. I grudgingly looked around, hoping something would just pop out at me. Eventually I bought a new pair of jeans and a shirt.

What vividly comes to mind when I think of that day was being unusually self-conscious that I was a size 10 and Samantha was a size 0. I was only 3 inches taller than her, but yet a size 10 versus her 0? Body type and sizes had never made an impression on me before. I vaguely recall wearing somewhat similar matching black shoes. In fact, our entire outfits matched, which wasn't uncommon for us. (We had matching attire for the Chicks with Sticks endeavor, which consisted of army green pants and homemade tie-dye shirts—very classy, I must say.)

Back at the house, preparing for our date, new clothing hanging on a hook hung over the back of the closet door, I took a shower. While in the shower, using my loofah, I remember thinking to myself *I better be extra clean in case I hook up tonight.* This is not a thought that had ever previously crossed my mind even with my previous boyfriends, and I don't know why it did this particular night. At age 19, I was still a virgin. Perhaps I was hoping to finally find true-boy-love and be swept off my feet by a romantic foreigner, since no one I had yet met had that effect on me? Perhaps I hoped Samantha and I would run off together after we realized we loved each other and not men? Hormones were pushing all kinds of thoughts through my mind.

We arrived at Brian's below-grade bachelor pad apartment, on the ground floor of a nondescript multi-apartment complex in Walden, sometime after dusk. After Samantha gave Brian an enthusiastic hello kiss, I met Brian's friend, Roland.

Roland, with his sandy brown hair, blue eyes, and skier's body, didn't look like the guys I usually met in Rhode Island. Being young and rather uncultured, I was impressed by his Swiss roots and foreign accent.

Most of the evening passed in a blur, and blurry it still remains trying to gather the details now, decades later. What I can recall is it was the four of us hanging out in the apartment for most of the night. The place was dark, but I don't think it was intentional mood lighting. At some point during the night, a few other women came over who, I believe, were neighbors.

We were offered drinks, but I could not tell you what those drinks were. I couldn't tell you if it was beer or a mixed drink because I paid no mind to it and just drank what they put in my hand. My eyes followed Samantha. I wanted to impress Samantha with my willingness to participate in whatever the night held. I certainly had a reputation for being a prude, so, for her, I was trying to branch out of my comfort zone.

We played card games and threw darts. I threw one dart so fast and far flung that it hit the wallpaper border of the kitchen to a chorus of rousing laughter and mock applause.

Somewhere after game time, after the neighborly women left, Brian made us dinner. Brian prepared steak, rice, and a vegetable. Samantha sat across from me and Roland was on my left. As Brian served dinner, he poured us another round of drinks. It had to have been mixed drinks because I didn't notice anything wrong with the flavor of the drink, but it is at that point that Samantha and I both believed we had been slipped a date rape drug. We debated for a long time after if this drug was slipped into our drink or into our food. Regardless, we were heavily drugged with no witnesses or anyone to come to our rescue that night.

After dinner, we must have started playing some game again, because the only thing I remember is that I was suddenly standing fully exposed across the table from Samantha and thinking, "Wow! Her bush is not the same color as her hair!" I remember feeling insecure standing naked at this table playing some game that involved stripping. I remember asking myself, "Should I have shaved? Or not? What is pubic hair etiquette?" Among the thousands of things Samantha and I talked and gossiped about, these things we did not discuss. (And yet, I can vividly remember the first day she tried a tampon, which didn't seem that far before this night, in hindsight.)

Fuzzy details float into view throughout the rest of that night. I woke up with blurry vision, half my body on the couch and half on the floor, with Roland penetrating me.

I must have decided to get out of there when the sun rose because I was squinting as I hopped around trying to get my leg into Samantha's jeans and couldn't, because they were size 0—the downside to purchasing matching jeans.

I found the right clothes and we eventually got back to Samantha's house where I spent the day throwing up rainbows of blue Gatorade and yellow Spanish rice in between sleeping and trying to remember and forget simultaneously.

My period was late that month and I thought I was pregnant. I had been raped, lost my virginity to a skier from Switzerland, *and* I thought I was going to be stuck with a baby!? Thankfully, my period arrived late, not without massive anxiety. My life felt like it just kept falling further off track.

After losing my virginity in a most inauspicious way, I stayed clear of men. I became even more of a prude and took on the protector role for my friends. Emily and Samantha were typical teenagers, a year older than me, and they were always trying to find dates. I was not interested. I had tried dating in high school. Nothing felt right—of the three guys I dated during and immediately after high school, I simply did not connect with any of them. After graduation, I was still disinterested in men, but not yet fully aware that I was interested in women. I just thought I preferred female companionship to male.

One day, post-high school graduation, as a result of one of our AOL chat room flirtation sessions, Emily persuaded me to go to Paulson, a city north of Princeton, to meet a few Jamaican men, one of whom she liked. At the time, I felt like they were so much older than us. They were probably in their thirties while I was 19 and Emily was 20.

We arrived at their apartment and the space seemed set up as a temporary stop on a journey. The furniture was hand-me-down, side-of-the-road chic. Not too many places to sit, so at first, we all squeezed in together on the couch. The two men brought us drinks and, as uncomfortable as I was, I drank too much, too fast. Still, my instincts put me on alert and I could sense the situation was going to get ugly. I had enough forethought to put my keys in the fake palm tree planter in the living room.

Emily disappeared into the only other room in this small, sparsely furnished apartment with the man she had wanted to see. I must have been in and out of an alcohol blackout because I came to awareness as I was being

groped and literally being face-sucked by the friend. He was not that tall—
maybe 5'7"—and not that overpowering in size since he was rather lanky. But
somehow, with the Jamaican thrumming music banging in my brain and the
alcohol in my system, his mouth overtook mine and sucked me in. His teeth
were a mess—he was missing his canines and when his lips fully encased my
small mouth and tried to bring my tongue into his mouth, all I could think
was, "Eeeww ... he's so gummy!"

I remember when I touched his skin, probably to push him away, he was
moist, dewy, but not really sweating. It made me want to run. He pulled me
into a dance, capturing me as he was gyrating, grinding his body against mine
to the drumming beat of the music.

I was manipulated into the single bedroom where Emily was already with
her guy. The mattress was on the floor with nothing but a top sheet and when
this guy pushed me down, I fell forever in slow motion, like the bad dream
scenes you see in movies where people fall and fall and fall forever, flailing
about, mouths agape in silent screams.

The guys had their hands all over our bodies. As drunk as we were, I don't
know what kind of consent we provided. It was dark and they didn't want us
leaving the bedroom.

I was groped all over and soon felt fingers going for my pants—I pushed
and shoved and finally rolled off the mattress onto the floor.

Before he could reach me again, I feigned an excuse for needing to get up
and turn the light on. I told them I had to call Samantha, so she could come
join the fun.

Samantha could hear my nervous, panicky tone on the phone and left
work to drive in her signature NASCAR style in her red Mazda to come rescue
us. It took about 20 minutes for her to arrive. I don't recall what happened
between the time I called her and the time she finally arrived. Samantha
knocked loudly when she arrived, and I drunkenly threw myself at her and
told her where I hid the keys to my Jeep Wrangler. We grabbed Emily and
high-tailed it out of there in my car, never to see those men again. We went

back the next day to pick up Samantha's car, which was hidden from the guys, having been parked around the block.

I was date raped at 19 and I never reported it. I didn't know I could (or should). I was date raped, drunk as I was, by men old enough to know better. Until now, I've kept these stories primarily private.

My life has been filled with hiding. I had a sister with mental illness, a home I was embarrassed to show to friends, a mother who drank too much, sexual interest in one of my best female friends, a birth mother and an adoptive mother, and then my traumatic entry into womanhood. Long after these experiences, I will have many other challenges I keep hidden from the world. Revealing my truth only to a selected few.

Aside from the fact that I will never be able to tolerate the taste of blue Gatorade—not because of the flavor but for what it symbolizes—my life carries on. I often wonder if I can be the full expression of myself when I carry so many secrets? Can anyone?

Jamie was my first girlfriend. We met in 2001 on a gay dating website. Online dating was new to the world and searching through a computer seemed like a safer option for seeking a same-sex partner than to go looking in public. I wasn't ready to out myself to my family or at work. I was curious to see if this is what I wanted—if this was who I was.

I met Jamie in the lobby of her dorm. She was short, like me, and had long brown hair. I wasn't head over heels attracted to her, but I was very curious and nervous. The only person I had been really sexually attracted to, up to this point, was Samantha. But since she was straight and I was coming to realize I was not, I repressed anything I had felt toward her.

Here I was at 19 and enamored with the idea of being with a woman for the first time. It was a bold step for me. I didn't know how to be with a woman. I didn't know what sexual attraction to a woman would feel like.

Jamie was unstable and emotionally abusive almost from the get-go. Though we stood eye to eye, she had experiences and knowledge with women that I didn't have, so I dealt with it. I did not know there was a better way to be in a relationship. I had not been treated with respect growing up, so I had no concept that I was worthy of respect, affection, or love. What was love? I was on my mission to break away from my mother and sister. That was my goal for this relationship.

When we met, I was living in Rhode Island and Jamie was going to school at Boston University. She would come to visit me in Rhode Island and I would go to visit her in Boston.

When Jamie came to visit me, we stayed in my room at the recently rebuilt house on the same lot where I grew up. I had left Samantha's after a year of bunking there and moved back with my mother and sister to the new four-bedroom, two-and-a-half-bath house. Within weeks of my family moving in to a fresh, clean, modern house, it was no less cluttered than the original house. We had fewer things because of the fire, but somehow the house still was in constant disarray, except for my room, of course. It was like my mother and sister's minds were frenetic, which translated to the physical space that surrounded them. I had nothing for my sister to steal anymore as I kept my most important things with me all the time, carrying them in a backpack I kept in the car. But I still locked my room. Habit. And my sister still broke in. Habit.

While back at school, attending the local community college and in the midst of determining which four-year school I wanted to transfer to, the most important priority was to get me far enough away from my mother and sister that I didn't have to live with them any longer. I was debating between a handful of New England colleges. Eventually I selected Salem State in Massachusetts for three reasons: 1) because it was close to Jamie, 2) because I loved the diversity of Salem and had always been interested in witches, Wicca, and Paganism. And if those weren't good enough reasons because 3) my favorite colors were blue and orange and those were the school's colors. Despite my superficial reasons for choosing it, it really was an amazing school and an amazing experience.

After a few months of secretly dating Jamie, Amanda caught on. She was about 14 at the time. Since I was back in the house, Amanda was back to her old habits of breaking into my room. Despite having locked all the locks on my bedroom door, my sister barged in on Jamie and me in bed one afternoon. We were wrapped together in the sheets of my captain's style platform waterbed and before I could roll my way off the floating waves of my mattress to try to convince Amanda what she was seeing was not was she was seeing, she was off to tell my mother. I had no warning, no time to prepare what I wanted to say—nothing. They had arrived home earlier than I had planned and the carpet was pulled out from under me and I was thrust in fight or flight mode—yet again.

I had already come out to Maria and my four closest friends at this point, which had only been a couple of months before. Coming out to my mother was a very difficult thing, followed by sharing this news with the rest of the extended family. My mother and I were already on shaky ground since I had found Maria and was spending so much time with a "mother" who was not her. I needed more time to delicately break the news to her, but instead the experience was riddled with strife. My mother needed time to grieve the loss of what she knew and what she expected for my life.

First, my mother thought she would lose me to my birth mother when I was 18 and now, at 19, she was worried she would lose me to a world she knew nothing about. Telling Maria I was gay before telling my mother didn't help the situation. Once my mom had time to process (quite a bit of time),

I am happy to say, she came around. Amanda did not destroy me as she had likely hoped.

I enrolled at Salem State for the spring semester and lived in the dorm for my first semester. I was absolutely miserable. I felt like an outsider and my roommate was bizarre—a sleeps-with-an-8-inch-knife-under-her-pillow type of eccentric. I was able to get in-state residency for my tuition, which brought my tuition down to a slightly more reasonable amount of money, but I lived off student loans and worked two jobs. Working over 40 hours a week while also being a full-time student made me different from many of my classmates who did not have to earn money to survive.

While being gay was far more open and accepted in Salem than in small-town Rhode Island, I was still a minority. I was the token lesbian on the floor of my dorm. I was free from home for the first time and I wanted to be who I was, unapologetically. My contrarian nature took over and I went out of my way to make my dorm room "look gay," because I felt like my physical appearance didn't look the part enough. It was this odd conflict of wanting to be who I was and yet wanting to not be who I was, which was a common pattern for me.

At some point, while seeking my place in the world, an identity without my family, I put an Irish Pride rainbow bumper sticker on my newly acquired, used red Saturn. It was a bittersweet day I traded in my dad's Jeep for a car with better gas mileage—something my broke college self needed desperately. Within weeks of putting that sticker on, my car was broken into at the school parking lot as well as at a train station. It was then that I realized displaying any type of pride externally wasn't a good idea. The break-ins could have been unrelated to my Irish Pride sticker, but I took the sticker off my car and never put any on after that—and my car was no longer vandalized.

After dating for a year, Jamie and I moved in together so I could get off campus. We both applied for summer jobs at a well-known tourist destination in Boston. I got the job. Jamie did not. She resented me every day for it. I believe this was partly the beginning of the end of our relationship, even though we stayed together for several years after this. Our relationship had always been rocky. I, a more confident individual, and she, exceptionally insecure, were the relationship equivalent of oil and water.

Working at this new job opened my eyes to the diversity of life and people. I had so many coworkers who were gay and it was amazing to be surrounded by that rich experience for the first time in my life.

Jamie and I broke up. We got back together, broke up, got back together again. It was a nasty, self-doubting cycle. She kept having affairs and I would keep taking her back. I felt, at the time, that I needed her to make a new start, away from what I knew as home. After nearly five years we broke up. This time it stuck.

Age 23

In 2004, I graduated college with a degree in communications. Before having my final break with Jamie, having no reason to remain in the Boston area after graduation, when Jamie asked if I wanted to move to Connecticut, I said yes. Her aunt had a house that she was looking to rent out inexpensively and we could certainly use the break from the high rent prices of Salem.

As I prepared to move from Boston's North Shore, I boldly searched for a job in marketing to break away from manufacturing and retail. My interest in marketing began when I started collecting and analyzing alcohol ads from magazines in middle school with Erica. I had been fascinated by how well the industry knew its market and was able to target customers. I secured a marketing position in the insurance industry and was excited to be at my first desk job.

One day, my new coworker, Maya, said something to me that assumed I had a boyfriend. I had only been on the job for a couple of weeks and our conversations had consisted primarily of small talk. When Maya assumed I had a boyfriend, I didn't correct her.

This was the first time I "covered" my identity at work. Covering is essentially when you hide some aspect of your identity for fear of political or social consequences. Many people walk a fine line in revealing who they are when making new friends, especially at work.

In this case, friendship with my cubical mate, Maya, developed very quickly, despite my hiding something important about my life. It was at least a month before I finally got up the nerve to come out to her. It felt difficult, primarily because quite a bit of time had passed without me clarifying things.

Politically, I knew that my being a lesbian was not going to impact her in any way whatsoever, but I worried about hurting her feelings. I didn't want her thinking I didn't trust her enough to tell her about my life. I wrestled with how to tell her and then, one day, I just did. She was caught by surprise, but we laughed about it and we moved on. Fortunately for both of us, she understood and we have remained best friends for over 16 years.

All in all, it took me about a month before I felt comfortable enough to share my true identity with one coworker—just *one* person—one out of my one hundred colleagues. I had an uneasy feeling from my first day on the job. I couldn't put my finger on it, but it was there.

I eventually heard through the rumor mill that, within a few days of starting my job, speculation began about me. My boss, a director at the company, was overheard stating that I had the "captain of the softball team lesbian look" about me, which sadly wasn't far off.

Like most workplaces, my company had a large number of people who thrived on spreading gossip and being involved in other people's drama. I had surface relationships with the people at the core of the gossip and drama. I didn't want to be outright standoffish, but I also didn't want them to think it was okay to share people's business with me. I surely wasn't going to share any of my personal life with them.

It didn't take long before my work environment became toxic. Instead of hearing the nasty comments directly from the gossip group, I would overhear things in passing. There was the time I heard a claims representative comment that the customer on the phone "sounded like a faggot" or another time someone from accounting said a coworker looked like a dyke. People think nothing of making comments like this, showing off ingrained prejudices and the way they stereotype people. My workplace began to feel dangerous. I knew *no one* else could know anything about me.

This was uncharted territory for me. In my countless jobs, I had never, ever heard such hateful things directed toward LGBTQ+ people. The striking contrast of being free and open to being thrust into a gossip-filled workplace, where talking behind people's backs and being cruel to one another was the norm, felt so foreign to me. This was not what I had in mind when I left retail to pursue a "professional" office job. Even at the factory, this kind of hateful talk was not evident.

Age 24

In 2005, I was single, still living in Connecticut, and felt a bit out on the ledge alone. I had a handful of incredible friends, I was busy with work, but desired to be in a relationship. I reconnected with a former friend, Lindsay, on a popular dating website. We knew each other while I was growing up. I was friends with her sister and we had all gone to high school together. She was still living in our hometown.

After surviving Jamie, meeting Lindsay with such an amazing, upbeat, sunny personality was great. Lindsay was the exact opposite of Jamie in every single way possible. She was warm, loving, and funny. Lindsay was a free spirit and had an artist vibe about her. She had a zest for life that brought lightness to my life that I'd never felt before. I was entranced with her and addicted to how I felt when I was with her. I couldn't wait to hold her, kiss her, or just be near her. I looked forward to leaving work behind me so I could enjoy time with Lindsay. My life had totally flipped around. I was happy. What a concept!

My mom and sister loved Lindsay (not that this influenced my opinions). They had hated Jamie (without exception *everyone* in my life hated Jamie).

Lindsay was empathetic and compassionate—two things I hadn't had for the previous five years with Jamie. Lindsay and I had been dating for close to a year when, one day when we were in Rhode Island, we had stopped by my mom's house to say hi and ended up staying for dinner. It was an impromptu visit and my mom was visibly drunk. While we were standing in the doorway about to leave, my mom peed her pants in front of the both of us. I heard the sound of pee hitting the floor before I realized what was happening. I was embarrassed on levels that are indescribable. We got into Lindsay's Toyota and I cried. I was so mortified. My mom was so drunk she had no idea she even did it the next day, nor did she seem to have any level of embarrassment. Lindsay let me sob. She didn't judge me. She didn't assign my mother's behavior to me—a fear I carried my entire life.

Age 25

During the time Lindsay and I were together, my sister—at the age of 20—had her first child, Alyssa. I was sitting at my desk at work when I got the phone call that my sister was in labor. I looked at my cubical mate, Maya, and said, "I gotta go." I arrived at the hospital sometime in the afternoon and Lindsay met me there. Seeing Alyssa, looking into that baby's pure little face, somewhere in the pit of my stomach, the bottom of my being, I *knew* that I would one day raise my niece. With my sister's history of irresponsible behavior, it already felt like a fact.

No one was happy that Amanda became pregnant. And, while my sister was old enough to have and raise a child, we all knew from the start that any child born to her would encounter some kind of danger. And yet, somehow, Amanda appeared to have pulled herself together just a little bit and seemed to be okay during this time—this was short-lived.

My spending time with Lindsay in Rhode Island meant I was able to spend a lot of time with Alyssa while she was a baby. Lindsay and I were the doting aunts. We were both in the hospital the day Alyssa was born and we were there for all the milestones.

I almost moved back to Rhode Island to be with Lindsay. I spent most of my weekends at her place there even though I was the one who lived alone and she shared the in-law apartment with her grandmother in the basement of her childhood home. Somehow being enmeshed with Lindsay's family on my visits didn't bother me too much. She had a close-knit family, something I yearned for.

I bought my first condo in 2007, in Connecticut, while Lindsay and I were still dating. I asked for her input, which she didn't offer. This purchase meant I hit my huge goal of owning a home by the age of 25. Unfortunately, I bought this townhouse in the worst possible economic environment just before the crash. When I set a goal, I achieve it, whether or not it's in my best interest at the time.

Lindsay was angry when I turned over the deposit and signed the paperwork on the condo because I had "planted the flag in the sand" in essence, saying that I was staying in Connecticut with or without her. We broke up shortly thereafter.

In truth, the final straw that broke the camel's back in our relationship was not the condo purchase but when I found out Lindsay was giving my sister money. I lost it. I felt this to be the ultimate betrayal because Lindsay knew, even more so than anybody, how damaged my relationship with my sister was. Lindsay had deliberately gone behind my back to give my sister money, knowing how I would react.

Lindsay knew my sister's character; she had witnessed a lot of the "craziness" in my house, just from growing up near us. I felt she should have known better. Over the years Lindsay and I were together, Amanda and Lindsay talked. Amanda could be persuasive and a charismatic manipulator of Lindsay's emotions. The money Lindsay was giving to my sister was presumably being used for Alyssa, but in reality, based on what I could see, it was for a litany of inappropriate behaviors that had nothing to do with my niece.

I am certain that Lindsay believed she was doing what she felt was in Alyssa's best interest. Truthfully, my tolerance level for any empathy toward Amanda and her antics was nonexistent. I was so angry that Lindsay didn't understand that she was a pawn in my sister's game. Unlike leaving Jamie, who treated me far worse for far longer, this betrayal of loyalty to my sister over me was too much for me to forgive, and I painfully moved on.

PART V
DIAGNOSIS

Age: 27-30

July 2008-July 2011

Age 27

Alyssa had been born in 2006. When word got out that Amanda was pregnant again, it was an ugly scene across the board. No one was supportive. When Alyssa was born, for the most part, everyone rallied around realizing it was in the best interest of the baby to be supportive of Amanda; myself included.

In July 2008, my nephew Jackson was born. When Jackson was born, there was no pomp and circumstance. There was no excitement. My mother was disgusted by the fact that Amanda had another baby. When Jackson was born, no one knew who his father was. As much as I hated my sister, I was still having a nephew.

When I got the call that Jackson was born, I rushed to the hospital. At first, my mother refused to go. Eventually, I convinced my mother that it wasn't fair to Jackson for his grandmother to not be there, so she acquiesced.

My sister, in her early twenties, was a mother of two with no job, no home of her own, and a constant rotation of irresponsible boyfriends.

Amanda lived in a backyard apartment with her boyfriend David when Jackson was born. Opening the front door into a cluttered living room revealed pills colorfully strewn around like confetti on the floor and uncovered, unprotected sharp objects on tables and in the kitchen. A child crawling about could easily have eaten these colorful "candies" or gotten cut on a jagged edge. I wanted to scoop up these babies and run away with them. My heart broke into pieces every time I left and didn't have them with me.

Amanda told us that David was Alyssa's father. Later, we learned that David was actually Jackson's father and happened to be around when Alyssa was born so Amanda, to keep things simple, had told us David was the dad. Later, while we were making court decisions involving parental care, we discovered through DNA testing that Alyssa's father was someone else.

At some point, Amanda and David were kicked out of the backyard apartment and moved over to my mother's house for a while. They stayed there until David disappeared and a new partner swept Amanda away to yet another unsuitable home, where she proceeded to produce yet another baby just 10 months later—Chloe. Three kids with different dads, all within four years.

Chloe's father was my sister's drug-addicted, physically abusive boyfriend at the time. Eventually, Chloe, Alyssa, Jackson, Amanda, and her boyfriend were living at my mother's house. The place was crowded and noisy.

After Lindsay and I broke up, I declared that I was going to be a crazy cat lady alone in my rocking chair with my homemade afghan (a gift from Maria). I felt very good about this decision and had determined that my cat, Remy, and I were destined to a life of freedom untethered from the drama and bull-shit of the women in our life. I had taken about two years off from dating and was genuinely enjoying my time alone.

When I thought I might be ready for company and someone to hang around with and realized being a spinster with cats wasn't the best future path for someone so young, I got back on an online dating website and met Victoria.

Victoria was ambitious like Jamie, intelligent like Jamie, but had a very soft and loving side like Lindsay. It felt like the perfect combination of traits that I was looking for in a woman. I was entranced by her long dark hair, her soulful eyes, and a spirit of calm that emanated from her. I wanted to touch her from the minute I saw her. She drew me in.

Since I had come out a decade earlier, I had been putting into the Universe, albeit on a surface level, that I wanted to be with an athletic, long-haired brunette—and here she was. I felt things for Victoria that I had not felt for anybody before.

We didn't share any common friends even though, we soon discovered, for two years we had lived a mile away from each other. I think one of the appealing things about meeting Victoria was that we didn't have any mutual ties (no dramatic lesbian connections), so we could just be us. Victoria didn't have any baggage. And I genuinely believed I didn't have any baggage—disassociation at its finest.

Victoria was a special education teacher and understood kids. She had an educated listening ear and let me talk about the whole messed up situation with my sister. By then, I had been spending regular time with Alyssa and Jackson, getting them out of the house and taking them fun places, making sure they had good food, clothing, and a peaceful night's sleep.

Victoria and I had our first date on a Sunday, at the chain restaurant LongHorn Steakhouse, at 2 o'clock in the afternoon. We knew we were somehow kindred spirits, since passing the afternoon in an emptyish chain restaurant seemed like a good idea to both of us. We stayed until the restaurant closed that night at 10 p.m. We drank a *lot* of diet cokes and occasionally ordered some food so they wouldn't chase us out. After our first date, I called Maria on my way home and declared, "She's the one," something I had never done or said before.

Victoria and I hung out at my townhouse that Tuesday night and then I saw her again later in the week. I told her I was having my niece and nephew for the weekend. "But, you're welcome to hang out; I don't know what we're doing yet," I offered. I fully expected her to say, "It's okay, I'll see you during the week." But she didn't say that. She said, "Sure."

That Friday, I had both kids with me. A total shit show of a scene. A clear demonstration that I didn't know how to care for two kids by myself. Victoria was my savior, our savior. She was the perfect person to be dropped into my life at that time. Something so simple, but so profound, was that she offered to bring me dinner that night. I'm certain she could sense I was in over my head. I hadn't held a baby until I was about to turn 19—that says it all.

I have a very fond movie in my head of Victoria walking into my town-house and seeing Jackson on the couch, 10 months old, completely unsupervised, and Alyssa on the floor pulling tissues out of the box. Immediately, she scooped Jackson up into her arms. I said, "All things considered, they're still safer here than where I just picked them up from." She fell in love with my unconventional family. As a result, this pushed us into an important conversation very early in our relationship.

With Jackson in her lap and Alyssa playing by her feet, I told Victoria, "I don't know when, I don't know how, I don't know what the logistics of this are, but they are going to be my kids. I know that deep within my being. So, if you want to be with me, you just need to know that they kind of come with the package." In my mind, I imagined having Jackson dropped back into my lap and Victoria walking out the door. Instead, she just nodded in agreement. And that was that. She is a woman of few words, which I found quite appealing, at first.

And from that first week on, we were taking care of Alyssa and Jackson on weekends. (Later, when Chloe was born, she stayed with Amanda or her paternal family.) Victoria and I "dated" on the two-hour car rides to and from Rhode Island to bring the kids to my townhouse in Connecticut. Our social life had a "children factor" built in from day one. It seemed like the situation was complicated, but the relationship and us working together was so natural and easy. If there was anything at all against Victoria, it was only that when I told my mother we were getting married, she was distraught that I was marrying a Yankees fan. Growing up in a die-hard Red Sox household and state, this *was* a big deal to her.

Victoria and I went on our first date in March during the time I was still working my insurance job despite my unsettled feelings. Getting my work life organized was a challenge but I was pleased with the way things fell into place. At home, things were all-consuming.

All summer, we had been driving two hours each way from Connecticut to Rhode Island to pick the kids up after work on Fridays and return them on Sunday nights.

We had to reconfirm exactly where to pick up the children each week and we never knew what we would find. We'd arrive at the trailer park/back-yard apartment/someone's home/garage/my mother's house and be met with hungry children not wearing shoes; not changed or bathed; skin, nails, and hair showing poor hygiene habits; with bags under their eyes from lack of sleep—and we'd bring them to our home. They would sleep at our house for 20 hours at a time because they hadn't properly rested since we last saw them a week before. We'd feed and bathe them and go out for fun family activities all together. And then, when we'd finally settled in and the kids looked like kids should look, we'd morosely get back into the car to spend four hours driving back and forth to return the children to whichever location my sister called "home" that particular Sunday night.

For six months, Victoria and I were living together, part-time parenting together, and "dating" simultaneously. Not your traditional courtship by any stretch of the imagination.

Victoria was on summer break from school and we knew it would be a reprieve for Alyssa and Jackson to have some sense of stability and we knew Amanda wouldn't pass up the opportunity to be childless for a few weeks, so we planned for Alyssa and Jackson to stay with us for a full two weeks in August.

At the beginning of our two-week staycation with the kids, I was carrying a vacuum cleaner up the stairs with one hand, over my shoulder, and had a laundry basket in the other hand. The vacuum was heavier than I thought and trying to balance walking up the stairs with my hands full caused my hand to bend backward all the way. Several bones made this awful snapping sound. Pain followed. An emergency trip to the doctor, X-rays, and lots of patience followed that. And that is how I had a broken hand on the first day of the kids being with us for two weeks—poor Victoria!

For two weeks, we lived in our townhouse to see what it would feel like to be a family. It was fine. Except that it was pretty clear that something "wasn't right" with Alyssa. She would scream for hours and hours on end from her pack n' play bed that we set up in the living room. It was nonstop screaming and there wasn't much we could do to stop her. Comfort her. Hold her. Feed her. Rock her. The one thing that would get her to settle a bit was a specific *SpongeBob Square Pants* DVD. It was the DVD my sister used in lieu of watching her child. Amanda would put Alyssa in a car seat in front of a screen and play *SpongeBob*.

On the weekends, Alyssa's screaming was not super-alarming. We looked at the situation like having a colicky baby ... but Alyssa was three. Over the two-week staycation, we realized things were more troublesome than we first thought.

Age 28

Alyssa's developmental delays were obvious, especially to Victoria who saw this kind of thing in her classroom and took classes about it for her master's degree and continuing education. Alyssa preferred to express herself with vocalizing cries, using very few words. She called me Auntie Hen, instead of Jenn. And Victoria was Auntie Vee, instead of Victoria. Later, we would become Mom Jenn and Mom Vee. It wasn't until she was three that Alyssa formed her first sentence, somewhat incoherent, translated to (we think), "Shut the door, the cat is going to get out."

Almost at the end of our two weeks together, having settled into a nice daily rhythm and having had enjoyed a few fun day trips, the kids were well rested, happy, and healthy-looking, and dressed in clean clothes, when we got a panicked phone call from Amanda.

"Jenn, you've got to bring the kids back right now!"

"Why? They're good. They're happy. We still have a little more time with them!"

"No, no, no. You have to bring them back right away or you could be arrested!"

"What? Why? What are you talking about, Amanda?"

"The kids aren't allowed to be out of the state."

"I don't understand. We've had them all these weekends and they've been here for two weeks, why all of a sudden?"

"I don't have time for this! Get the kids back here right NOW! I'm at the hospital and CPS [Child Protective Services] is coming to see the kids. They need to be back at my place when CPS gets there."

"Okay. Calm down, Amanda." I turned and said to Victoria, "Start packing up the kids. We have to go back right now. I'll explain when I'm off the phone." And Victoria raised her hands in a questioning motion asking, "What?" I made a circling motion with my hands, to mean "Move, move, move ..."

Back to Amanda, "Okay, we're packing up the kids, tell me the whole story ..."

"I choked on a chicken bone and had to go to the emergency room. I forgot that CPS is coming to check on the kids. I'm under investigation ..."

"WHAT?" I interrupted "Why?"

"Never mind that, I'm not supposed to let the kids go out of state. I need the kids to be at the campground where we're staying by the time CPS gets there. Can you do that? Can you just get the kids there right away? I can't lose my kids, Jenn. I need you to do this!"

"You know, Amanda," laced with a little sarcasm, "If you would have told us this a few months ago when we planned this little vacation, we could have planned to stay in Rhode Island during this time!"

"I don't need this, Jenn. Just get the kids back here!" she pleaded, sounding exhausted and angry at the same time.

"We'll be there," I said.

More calmly, she gave me the address and location of the campground. She told me what I could expect when I arrived and then she hung up the phone.

Victoria and I were in a panic driving two hours to get the kids back before anyone knew they were out of state illegally. They were asleep in the back seat when we began a quiet discussion about what we wanted to do.

"We should talk about this," Victoria said seriously. (Although this was not the first time we had this conversation.)

"I know. This is getting ridiculous. I don't understand this whole inter-state thing. No one ever said this was a problem before. What do we want to do?"

"Do you want to try to get the kids away from your sister?" Victoria asked.

"I think so. I don't trust her with the kids. But if we do, how would we do it?" I asked.

"I think we need to prove that Amanda is an unfit mother. We need to make a case that the kids would be better off with us," Victoria proposed.

"Okay." And I thought for a minute. "I don't think we'd have a problem. We just tell this CPS person what we've seen every time we go to get the kids, right?"

"I suppose. It's not going to be easy, Jenn. Are you sure you want to get into this fight with your sister? Where would your mother be in all of this?"

"I think my mother knows that Amanda is not fit to be a mother. She never was happy when Amanda was pregnant. I think she would be on our side. I think."

Our conversation went back and forth with how we would build a case. And then, as we got closer and the kids were stirring awake, I asked Victoria, "Are we doing this? Are we going all in?"

She answered seriously, "You know, once we do it, we can't go back. Are you sure you're ready for this?"

I thought for just a minute. Nodded my head and said, "I'm in. Let's do it. These kids need us!" And we held hands until the kids were awake and we were pulling into the campground/trailer park where Amanda told us to go.

CPS was supposedly meeting us at the campground to see the kids and talk to us. Amanda had told them that we had taken them out for the day, omitting the fact that we were in a different state.

Victoria and I had made our decision in the car, so when Ellen, the CPS agent, came walking down the road, crunching gravel under her sensible shoes, we knew we were going to tell the truth, realizing that this would look like we were throwing Amanda under the proverbial bus (or in this case, camper) to protect the kids. My racing heart was pounding in my ears.

As we got out of the car, we could see that the campground drop-off address Amanda gave us was untidy and not suitable for kids. The camper was beat up, splinters were everywhere, and disgusting rotting water was evident. We got the kids out of the van and Alyssa ran off, oblivious to the dangers around her. Jackson started playing at the bottom of a tree minding his own business; just mindlessly sitting in the dirt, something he was familiar with doing unsupervised. We, to protect Amanda (or maybe ourselves) were nonchalantly pretending that we hadn't just been in Connecticut with them for two weeks. Fortunately, Chloe had been spending the day with her paternal aunt, so she wasn't there for this.

Ellen started asking us some questions and, heart still racing, I let loose some verbal diarrhea … sharing everything. I loved those kids so much and wanted them to have a great life. So, we went all in with every place we had been to pick up the kids, every person we saw, illegal things we had seen, to give Ellen the facts about what we'd witnessed and why we were concerned and wanted to do what we could to help the kids. My heart was heavy sharing this information with an official, knowing that I might be ruining my relationship with my whole family. But when you see something wrong, and you know there is a solution, how do you not do the right thing despite the ramifications?

That was in the end of August, and the kids were taken away within one week. We had been taking them every weekend for six months. Come September, the kids were removed from Amanda's care and—we were shocked—*not* given to us! This was not good, not what we planned when we had our discussion in the car. It seemed that we hadn't fully thought this out. We were out of state and, thus, out of consideration.

Because we lived in Connecticut and Amanda and the kids were Rhode Island residents, CPS said they legally couldn't grant us custody through typical kinship channels, but that we needed to obtain a Connecticut-issued foster care license. That's a complication Victoria and I didn't foresee. Now we had to start the foster care licensure process, which isn't known for its expediency.

The transition from the day Victoria and I spoke to the CPS worker to the day they took the kids a week later was not organized, caring, or thoughtful. They just came and knocked on the door, grabbed the kids and put them in different residences, cutting off any ties the kids had with each other. The CPS enforcement team took Chloe, the baby, immediately to Bethany, her paternal aunt, in the same town. Alyssa went with my cousin Becca, who had a foster care license and lived many towns away. And then Jackson was placed in a foster home with two gay men "somewhere" in Rhode Island. The three siblings were broken up—simply because Victoria and I lived in a different state than they did. Our guilt was intense.

As Victoria and I discussed our foster care license, we had to decide how many of the children we were going to foster. Victoria was always in favor of just taking the two we had been caring for on weekends. They knew us, we knew them, and we'd gotten things pretty well systemized at the house. But I was having a conscience battle about breaking up the siblings. Fortunately, Chloe was with Bethany, a blood relative. This fact ultimately eased my overwhelmed mind. Chloe was safe and in good hands with her father's sister.

On the way back from one of our many trips, we stopped at the beach. I had to hold back the deep desire to throw up while sitting on the wall of rocks facing the ocean—thinking how could I be the one to rip this family apart? This was my decision.

I was hoping Amanda would see the wisdom in Victoria and me raising Alyssa and Jackson. I was thinking she should be relieved since she wasn't able to provide a healthy environment. From my view, it seemed that Amanda cared more about her personal pleasure than the well-being of the little people she birthed.

As it turned out, that's not what Amanda felt. She was devastated. Horrified. She fought with every mothering basic instinct that remained in her body. She hung on to those kids as if they were the only thing that gave her life purpose—and I suppose that was true.

I had presumed CPS would keep Alyssa and Jackson together. I arranged for the kids (I thought) to stay with Becca so we would have access to them and be able to spend time together. Alyssa and Jackson were accustomed to spending time away from their mother, with their aunts.

However, Alyssa already had separation anxiety and attachment issues. Her reaction to separation from her mother, her weekend aunts, and her siblings did not make it easy for my cousin to manage. Alyssa was a ship without water and put on a show for Becca, featuring all her variations and colors of tantrums, nonstop screaming, and acting out. Becca did not do well with Alyssa. She made it just about a week before she could no longer subject herself or her own children to Alyssa's behaviors.

When Becca called tearfully to say she simply could not foster Alyssa anymore, I called our contact Sharon (one CPS level above the case worker Ellen) and yelled at her. I agreed that Chloe was fine with her father's family as Chloe didn't know her siblings and they didn't really know her. But, I told Sharon, you've got to keep Alyssa and Jackson together! PLEASE!

Sharon did not know what to do with me and said she'd call me back. She did not call me back. I called her back and was a protective mama bear on a tear because she had not provided us with an update. "This is unacceptable!" I ranted. Because yelling at someone to get what you want *always* works. (Not.)

However, Sharon was able to move Alyssa, so the two kids ended up together. They were both to stay with the foster dads, not given to Victoria and me. But at least the first hurdle was overcome. The kids were back together.

The foster dads "somewhere in Rhode Island" were only licensed for one kid and they were looking to adopt a boy. So now—surprise!—the boy has a sister and she was moving in. CPS had to rush a waiver through the system (with me calling hourly to get updates) to get the guys approved to foster two children. Our goal was to cut that red tape and get things processed, stat. We knew this would be in the best interest of the children.

Everyone I knew kept saying, "Just tell them you'll take the kids. Problem solved! What's so hard about that? Everyone wins! Kids stay with family they know!" Of course, that makes sense. But Connecticut and Rhode Island laws don't link on that level. They are not cooperative. This is common among different state agencies in regard to the welfare of children.

Victoria and I worked on getting through the reams of paperwork to complete, interviews, and inspections we had to pass. We needed to child-proof the house, which included smoke detectors in every room, carbon dioxide detectors on every floor, lead paint inspections, etc. to make the fostering license a reality. We were in production mode. My head was stuck on logistics.

While the kids were with their foster family, Victoria and I nested. We had been essentially living together/dating for six months. We were confident that we would be getting custody; it was just a matter of how quickly this was going to happen. We were hoping it was going to be a lot faster. We were adjusting our home for full-time children and we had to restructure the whole house so that everything fit.

Cleaning, clearing, organizing, and purchasing. We were filling the home with things we knew the kids would appreciate and love. Things they never got at their ever-changing temporary residences with their mother. We were buying their cribs and beds. We made a playroom out of the finished basement. With no time to waste, I was down in the basement ripping up the old carpet with my broken hand so we could lay in new carpet, paint the walls, and put up the kids' artwork up before their arrival.

In early November, about halfway through this process, I just quit my job without really thinking it through. Firstly, because it was a hostile and homophobic work environment and secondly, because we had the kids coming and it made the most sense for me to have more flexibility as a freelancer. Victoria, as a teacher, had no flexibility at all with her schedule and availability. I knew I wasn't supported at work and without buy-in I wouldn't get the flexibility of my schedule to make this new reality work. I knew I would figure out how to make money elsewhere—I wasn't concerned about that. Leap and the net shall appear.

We were impatient to get our foster care license—it took three months, which felt like three years. Despite never actually liking children or wanting to have my own, these kids meant the world to me and I was going to do everything I could to ensure that they had a good life.

Amanda had not left the picture or disappeared. She was sobbing all the time trying to figure out how to get her kids back. Some part of her brain knew that having Victoria and me get custody would be the only way she was going to be able to see her kids without major obstacles. Victoria, my mother, and I were able to help Amanda reach this logical conclusion. It was not Amanda's immediate conclusion—and given our sibling history, you can see why. She had hit the point where she must have realized she was *not* going to regain custody. Eventually, she started advocating for us to get custody of Alyssa and Jackson.

We officially got our foster care license the week of Christmas. It had been three months since we were permitted to see the kids. We had no idea how they were doing, other than me calling Sharon and saying, "We need an update. This is unacceptable," and getting perfunctory, "The kids are fine. The kids are healthy," sort of answers that told us nothing.

Once we confirmed our foster license approval, we were told it was okay to go get Alyssa and Jackson on Christmas Eve. We finalized the house, got ourselves together, and told our families and our roommate. This was the best gift we could ever have hoped for. We hoped the kids would think so too.

In that week leading up to our pick-up, I began to have guilty feelings about the two dads who were going to be losing their foster children at Christmas. This was the opposite of a great holiday for them. Unless they were totally ready to let the kids go. Maybe they had decided they didn't want the kids, right? It's not like Alyssa and Jackson were easy, after all. I was playing all sorts of justification games in my head. I was too elated to have finally won the licensure battle to really feel the pain of the other side. It wasn't the guys' fault. It was the broken system's fault. Of course, I told myself, the guys knew all along that the aunts from Connecticut were working on getting custody. Of course, right?

When we arrived to pick up the children, it turns out that CPS did not, at any point during the fostering period, tell the guys there were going to be aunts taking the kids eventually. Thus, when CPS notified these temporary dads, days before Christmas, that two aunts were coming to pick up the kids, we destroyed their world. The entire three months they had custody of Alyssa and Jackson, this couple had no idea that there were two people working to get custody. We later learned that they were fully planning to adopt both children even though they originally wanted only a boy. CPS had never even hinted to them that this was not a possibility for them.

I felt like the biggest piece of shit on earth knowing that we just ripped away their new family. Even though it wasn't our fault, it felt like it was our fault.

On a positive note for us, in the time this wonderful, loving couple opened their home to our children, they were able to get Alyssa potty-trained. And, before we arrived that day, they had written out extremely detailed instructions on all the things we needed to know about the kids. What they had learned, what they liked, things they had acquired, and what was special to them, etc. These guys were amazing. I couldn't stop the tears welling in my eyes because I felt so horrible about what was happening to them that day.

It was a really emotional parting. The guys had been talking to the kids about things in the future, like there was some permanency to the situation. We show up to take them away from this home they've now adapted to, from a loving environment where they presumably were happy, and the kids hadn't seen us in three months. The kids probably assumed they would never see us again. Understandably, they were confused, so they both screamed the entire two-hour ride home. It was brutal—gut-wrenchingly awful. Christmas, the following day, while joyous in our victory of having received custody, was terrible because the children's sadness was palpable to everyone around them. They were too young to articulate it, but everything about them was solemn.

Age 29

During the winter months, we found ourselves visiting Victoria's parents with the kids so we could build snowmen, play in the snow, and then curl up by the fireplace. Once it started to get warmer, we felt even freer, now able to hit up every local park and playground in the area. The kids would joyfully play on the slides and swings and were having a chance to just be kids, not panicking about where they would be sleeping at night.

Over the summer, we did typical fun outdoor activities, which included going to amusement parks like Six Flags and cookouts with friends. Those around us were really excited that we were making our dreams a reality and becoming this happy family.

We were doing everything we could to carefully curate a happy family vibe as our family struggles beneath the surface were already brewing.

While they kids couldn't tell us how much they were hurting, it was very visibly there. We learned very quickly that if we went out for any length of time, when we got back to the house, we would "pay the price."

At first it wasn't overly alarming. We would go out to play for a couple of hours and when we would come back, Alyssa would cry and be upset for at least the number of hours that we were out. She was only four at the time and did not have advanced verbal skills, so it wasn't easy getting to the bottom of what was making her upset. This continued every time we left the house, whether it was for something fun like visiting family or if it was for school. Once we got back to our house, in the safety of our four walls, she would let her guard down and wail.

Often, this was a guttural infantile cry, so it was hard to tell—is she hungry? Is she thirsty? Is there some particular toy she's trying to get? We never really knew.

As the months grew, her difficulties were becoming increasingly more apparent. The afternoon cries that would follow a great day playing at the park turned into crying through the evening, and eventually that turned into crying through most of the night.

Over time, the crying went from a basic needs cry you'd expect from any infant or toddler to a more indignant, rage type of wail. We were unable to find anything that soothed her from whatever was happening in her head that was causing her to be inconsolable. We would have to just let the crying run its course, which could be anywhere from two to six hours, depending on the time of day, what we had just done, what she may have just eaten (i.e., how much sugar), etc. We knew this wasn't typical behavior, but we also didn't know how exactly to address, fix, or coexist with it.

What we found to be a blessing (that we would later find out was a curse), was the fact that Alyssa was able to hold it together while we were out in public, including at functions with family members. She had enough self-control that she was able to avoid crying, screaming, or throwing a tantrum in public. But once we were in the safety of just the four of us, all the pent-up anger, sadness, and aggression would be unleashed on us, her family.

With limited mothering experience, I didn't know what to do, so I deferred to Victoria's special education training to navigate us through this. And I think, oftentimes, she felt stumped too. We were committed to finding solutions to whatever ailed our soon-to-be daughter.

It was part of our repertoire, at this point, that we knew if we were going to go out and have a fun family day and do something, we would be prepared for the wrath that would await us at the end of the day and into the night. This was a struggle specific to Alyssa. Jackson didn't exhibit any behaviors like this. He was one, turning two, and was a relatively quiet baby. Whether that was his natural state or he had to adapt that way because our resources and focus were often on quieting, calming, and soothing his sister, I am not sure.

When my sister demanded all my parents' attention, I would go outside or hide in my room and organize. Kids adapt, learn the work-around.

It took us a while to finesse Amanda's buy-in for the adoption. Based on our childhood and Amanda's persistent efforts to ruin, steal, or break everything I cared about, I'm confident that the thought of me having her kids was her worst nightmare. Little did Victoria and I know that once we eventually gained custody, the challenges would just be beginning.

After each meeting with Amanda, the kids would be visibly restless and unsettled. I would bring them to go see my mom. They thought Grammy was fun. She would always have treats for them. It was their reward after a difficult visit with their mother. And then I would bring the kids back home to Connecticut. In the car, the kids would usually sleep a little and then get to watch *Dora the Explorer* episodes and shows on a portable DVD player I hung on the back of the front seat. The two-hour drive back to Connecticut was melancholy most of the time. This took the entire Wednesday of every week for 78 consecutive weeks.

Once home, Alyssa's screaming fits increased on Wednesday nights and for a few days after. The amount of emotional turmoil she was in by seeing Amanda was devastating to watch—and being unable to fix this was painful. I hated not being able to find a solution.

Jackson, on the other hand, who was about 13 months old when he was taken from Amanda, hadn't bonded with her the way Alyssa had, so this process didn't seem as difficult emotionally for him. I think it was harder for him to deal with his sister's reaction to the visit than the actual visit itself.

As we approached the new year, entering 2011, Victoria and I finally swayed Amanda enough to where she was beginning to realize there was no chance she was going to get custody of her kids again. I planted the seeds that Victoria and I were the logical choice to parent her children. "Why would you want the kids to go anywhere else?" I would ask her. I told her that, with us as parents, she could still see the kids whenever she wanted. The kids would still see their grandmother and I promised to send her pictures.

With her acquiescing, when we had the open adoption agreement written, I showed Amanda that we wrote it in such a way that it was friendly to her. "This is an open adoption agreement and is *so* in favor of you! We would never want the kids to not have a relationship with you!" we enthused. We put in monthly visitation between the kids and Amanda as part of our terms. As long as she came to meet with the kids, we would continue to bring the kids for visits. It made sense to us. We thought it was a winning situation for all involved. Amanda, after much back and forth, finally seemed to agree.

The next step was to bring this agreement in front of the judge, have it approved, and then have all parties sign off on the arrangement. So, what day did the court choose for the hearing? Two days before our wedding. Naturally … it seemed nothing was ever going to go easy in this arrangement.

Age 30

On a summer Saturday in 2011, Victoria and I were scheduled to be married. And, as it turned out, we had to appear in Rhode Island two days before our wedding to stand in front of a judge about the adoption! We weren't 100% sure that Amanda was going to voluntarily sign her rights to us that morning. We feared she could still change her mind at the last minute and decide to keep fighting to get her children back.

The one clause our lawyer added that changed everything was about visitation. It was an open adoption where, if the birth mother misses two consecutive visits (and we dictate when and where all visits are), then she no longer retains any rights. It didn't matter if she had been caught using drugs, committing a crime, or anything else, none of that would invalidate the agreement. Only missing scheduled visits would do it.

If you were a mother fighting for your children, you would think that not missing visits was a positive thing. Why would you ever miss the chance to see your children, right? And that's what we pointed out to Amanda as we were sitting on the bench outside the courtroom waiting to see the judge.

At this point, David, Jackson's father (who had taken some part in raising Alyssa when she was young), had gotten involved. And Jake (Alyssa's dad), who was at the courthouse, had to sign over his rights as well and we didn't know what involvement he would want.

As it turned out, Jake was easy. Jake came to the courthouse, signed the papers, gave us his phone number in case we ever needed to reach him again, and left. One thing that didn't get complicated—we were so relieved.

David, on the other hand, had his girlfriend Anna (who was pregnant with their second child) and she was determined that David would be a stand-up dad to his son.

That day in front of the judge, Anna, for whatever reason, was not able to be at court. David didn't have Anna to tell him what to do or not do, so, when we clearly explained to David that it was in his and Jackson's best interest to sign the papers, he did. We never had any intentions of keeping David from seeing Jackson, regardless of what the adoption formally said. We had a good relationship with them, so our agreement with David and Anna was that we could plan time for the kids to hang out with them and get together, whenever they desired. They were good people caught in a complex and disagreeable circumstance. We had regular visits with them for about a year after the adoption was finalized. Over time, their priorities shifted to focus on their two little ones and they eventually stopped connecting with us to see Jackson.

The moments leading up to my sister signing the paperwork were some of the scariest moments of my life. After bouts of tears and questions, she finally signed the papers.

We waited for the doors to open for us to get in front of the judge. Everybody in the hallway was in agreement (finally), but there was still a chance the judge would not rule in our favor solely because Victoria and I were a lesbian couple and not yet married. Even if we had already been married, it wasn't a sure thing. In 2011, same-sex marriage was not yet legal in Rhode Island. And it would be another four years until it was recognized on a federal level.

We got lucky—the judge did not factor in the sexual orientation of those petitioning permanent custody and all was fine. He signed off on all the paperwork. We still had one last hurdle to get through, as the actual adoption hearing to finalize everything wasn't for a few months. But in that moment, all we wanted to do was celebrate as a newly minted family! We took a group photo in front of the judge and left the courtroom jubilant.

With the drama around getting the adoption papers signed, my wedding to Victoria seemed like a peripheral thing. I was high-strung dealing with the adoption and everything leading up to it. In hindsight, that wasn't fair to Victoria. I found myself saying the Serenity Prayer, "Grant me the serenity to accept the things I cannot change, Courage to change the things I can, And wisdom to know the difference." It repeated on a loop over and over in my head, despite my lack of religious convictions.

Once our wedding was over, we would have a few months until the hearing, so we focused on having a great wedding day!

Victoria and I had both ordered gowns online after the two of us had panic attacks walking into David's Bridal one day. Neither of us had any interest in wearing suits; however, we also had limited experiences in finding dresses.

We didn't know our dresses were coming from China until they arrived. Victoria's was deposited at our doorstep in a wooden crate with spiders and cobwebs—quite the sight! Mine came in a clean box, cobweb free! Mine fit perfectly and required no alterations. Victoria's dress, on the other hand, needed some work. Nothing major, but complicated to fix and fit it just right, so there was a lot of trying on and fixing before the big day, as well as triage during the big day by some skilled bridesmaids. Regardless of how we got there, my bride looked beautiful. The day was lovely, the yard looked perfect, and I couldn't have been happier to join together with my partner for life.

We opted for an intimate backyard wedding with about 70 guests. Like Julie McCoy on *The Love Boat*, I was accustomed to managing events, as I had been doing freelance work that required event planning for four to five events monthly. I was always the person with the clipboard giving clear instructions with step-by-step directions so people wouldn't make mistakes. That's how I approached our wedding.

I was able to negotiate with a wedding photographer, videographer, caterer, etc. and kept our costs lower because they were all business contacts of mine.

One of the funnier stories (which could have turned out disastrous) from the day involved our wedding officiant, who happened to be Connecticut's Lt. Governor. When she arrived, she had her security detail in tow and they went off to secure the area.

Meanwhile, one of the neighbors was planning a wonderful surprise … to set off celebratory fireworks in our honor. My maid of honor Maya's husband happened to overhear someone discussing the logistics and he said, "Doesn't someone want to alert the secret service that there are going to be fireworks?" Thankfully, that was handled, or we could have had a newsworthy incident at our wedding!

Both Maria and my mother were at my wedding. Amanda was not invited. My mom regularly used a cane for an ongoing foot problem. Maria had her foot in a boot cast from a recent injury. The two of them walking me down the aisle with the cane and the boot was another logistics challenge. We had to find just the right way to position them as I think I was propping them up more than they were walking me down the aisle. Honestly, the sight of two overweight women, similar heights, hobbling and holding onto me for stability was … hilarious. I still laugh about it when I happen to catch the video clips of the day, despite how these relationships subsequently turned out.

The thing that saddened me the most about my wedding day was that some invited family members chose not to be there because they didn't accept me or my "gay lifestyle." In particular, my favorite Aunt Debbie, who had been there for me my entire life and had helped me find my birth mother, declined our invitation. She simply didn't believe it was acceptable to marry a woman. I would be able to wrap my head around this argument if it was due to her religious convictions, but she was the least religious of my family members. My other aunt I half-expected to not partake in the festivities because of her deeply held religious beliefs, but she put them aside and was a proud aunt to both Victoria and me throughout the wedding and beyond. You never really know how people will show up in a given situation—it's interesting to let people surprise you.

We had a karaoke machine, as this was something Victoria loved doing. She sang the 14-minute version of 1980's Sugarhill Gang song, "Rapper's Delight" to kick off our wedding festivities after the ceremony, without needing the teleprompter! I told her, my new wife, that she would be divorced before the ink on the wedding contract was even dry if she tried to get me to come on our makeshift stage to sing with her. She acquiesced to my wishes. Instead, I was mingling around the tables, still in my white wedding gown, while she was up there singing her heart out.

Thankfully, unlike other special events yet to come in our life, our wedding, with picture-perfect summer weather, was a cheery, calm, and joyful celebration.

PART VI

DESPAIR

Ages: 31-34

August 2012-July 2015

Age 31

Every summer we went camping, starting in 2010. Most of our annual family camping trips had included some horrible interaction with other campers because, even though we would try to keep Alyssa as far away from every other camper as possible, others could inevitably hear her screaming or witness her fits around the campground. We were on guard and had to be prepared.

I had just left a busy week at a conference that was capped off by a confusing and enraging encounter with a coworker. I found myself in the middle of the woods with a shrieking child and realized I was not in the frame of mind to suddenly be camping. It was the polarity of going from being "on" for seven days straight in a business environment away from my kids and my chaotic life without having any transition time to being back to reality and dealing with my out-of-control child. This caused a mini-breakdown of sorts and I snapped and thought, "Nope, nope, this is never happening again."

From the campground, I pulled out my phone and emailed the folks I had just been with and essentially said, "I'm done. I will serve out my contract until you can find a replacement for me. How I was treated is unacceptable and I'm not letting anyone treat me this way again." I then stated that I was on vacation for the next week and would not be responding to any emails.

When we went camping, I didn't bring my laptop; we always locked our cell phones in the glove box of the car, as it was off-the-grid time. The objective was to connect with each other. Once I got the email out, that was it. Victoria was okay with my decision to leave the organization. Despite her rigid tendencies, she never questioned my decisions when it came to business, regardless of how risky it may have appeared. If I believed all was going to be fine, it would be. Victoria understood.

I had five days of camping and spent most of that focused on keeping Alyssa from having a meltdown that would clear the campground. When

I got home, I had a handful of new business opportunities surface, which, in my mind, further proved my decision was the best decision for me at that time and that I *didn't* need to allow people to treat me poorly to be successful.

At the end of the camping trip, when the kids and Victoria went to sleep, the car was unpacked, and the house was quiet, I had a chance to just stop and think. I had all this pent-up rage that I didn't know how to process. I decided, "I'm joining a gym." Considering that I was an athlete my entire life, it is odd that I had never actually exercised in a gym (other than the school gym). I always treated the outdoors as my gym.

In 2012 I weighed 168 pounds and was very unhealthy. I worked and took care of things at home for my family, was stressed to the max with child complications, and thus didn't pay attention to myself. At the time, I didn't think I was overweight, despite being a size 14 on a 5'3" frame. My confidence and my weight never had any relationship to each other, for which I am grateful.

Professionally, I was hitting every achievement marker I could possibly hit. That's where my confidence shined. But physically I was falling apart. I look at pictures of me from that time on my Facebook feed and cringe, but I don't remember feeling bad at the time—likely the result of disassociation, my lifelong go-to coping strategy. I remember a day in August where I was at my friend's house, we were at the pool, and the way my thighs rubbed together just snapped something in my brain—I had to do something to change this feeling.

The combination of feeling stressed about my daughter's unmanageable behavior combined with a career incident that felt offensive and out of control led me to do something I COULD control.

I joined a gym geared toward the 65+ crowd, which felt natural for me and was an obvious choice because it was not intimidating. I've always felt like a senior citizen at heart. It was $70 a month, which felt like an extravagance at the time. Especially when another gym just down the street was only $10 a month.

I was so anxious, nervous, and insecure—afraid I wouldn't know how to use the equipment the right way. I remember vividly sitting in my car texting with my best friend, Maya, about my anxiety level. Then I said, "Eff it, if I am going to do this, I need to take the first step and get my ass in that gym." And I did.

I set realistic expectations for myself and decided I was just going to walk on the treadmill while gaining my bearings in this new environment.

The purpose was focused very much on gaining much needed mental clarity at first. If I were just to give my mind an hour a day to focus on my health and well-being, then surely the rest would follow. My hypothesis was right. As I started to regain focus on the important things in life, such as my family and finding that delicate balance between business and being a mom and a wife, it all started to come together. I realized that having people in your life who are causing you unneeded stress and anxiety was not healthy and they needed to go. I was committed to making a change (mentally, emotionally, and physically) for my family and my business.

I first began by being very deliberate about not tolerating anyone who wasn't on board with the new direction of my life. There was no room in my life for friends, family, colleagues, or clients who were unsupportive naysayers. I had so much going on in my life that I couldn't handle any added negativity that wasn't serving some purpose. I put my foot down and got rid of the baggage people brought to the table.

I began setting goals for my physical well-being, which flowed into my business too. For over a year I simply walked—and walked—and walked. After walking for a while, I started to count calories and watch what I was eating. My goal was to take small and deliberate baby steps—one better decision each day around my health and well-being.

Once I achieved my initial goals, I started to get bored with the treadmill indoors. One beautiful day I said, "Why am I walking inside?" and went to the nature trail near my house and enjoyed walking outside for exercise, for the first time in a long time. I alternated between walking inside on crummy weather days and outside on nice ones. While the idea of kicking it up a notch to running while I power walked kept popping into my head, on a related note, I began to rekindle a long-time friendship with Carolina, a childhood friend, who still lived in my hometown.

When Jackson and I needed to escape the frenetic energy that Alyssa was setting off in our house, we would visit Gram Maria and Papa Gary (Maria's husband) in Rhode Island. Carolina (who lived about 10-minutes away from my birth mother) and I would spend time together while Jackson visited with his grandparents. He had no idea of how dysfunctional all of this was, as this was all he knew since he was a baby. His world, all of ours, orbited around Alyssa's mental health needs—in the same way my world orbited around my sister's when we were growing up, and I didn't know the difference.

Carolina and I were having drinks at the beach one afternoon and while my inhibitions were down, I said aloud what had been percolating in my mind, "We should run a marathon." Carolina, with equally questionable judgment in that moment, blindly followed along and said, "Yeah, let's run a marathon!" After sleeping on it, we came to our senses. "Maybe we'll run a half marathon first. Let's be a little more realistic."

Running, in so many ways, changed my life. It gave me structure, purpose, and goals to work toward. It also gave me a justifiable reason to physically flee my house when things were really starting to heat up with Alyssa's increasingly worsening behaviors.

What started out as a need for mental clarity to get a better handle on my life (which felt like it was falling apart), turned out to be the start of a new habit, which I believe saved my life. And the side benefit is that I went from a size 14 to a size 4.

Age 32

About a year after I started training, in fall of 2013, Carolina and I registered for our first race to be run in November of the following year. We wanted sufficient time to train for a half-marathon (13.1 miles). We chose Walt Disney World to run our first race—primarily because Carolina is a die-hard Disney fan and I was indifferent as to where we ran (as long as I was out of my house).

Before we flew to Florida, we decided we should test ourselves by running a 5K (3.1 miles) first; a training event. The goal was to get a sense of pace and what any semblance of running together as a pair would feel like. Carolina is 5'7" compared to my 5'3", so we assumed pace matching would be challenging based on the length of our strides alone. It was amazing that we were able to run at the exact same pace for training and race days. Even if she or I felt like either of us could be running faster, we kept the same consistent pace because running for any length of time alone is boring.

I found it beautiful to be outside for three or four hours (depending on where we were training). Either Carolina would come to me or I would go to her—a two-hour drive between us—on weekends. Either she would stay at our house or I would stay overnight at her house and then we would do our run in the morning. It took a lot of planning to get our combined training sessions organized but it was better than sitting in the house listening to Alyssa scream. I had to run. Carolina was someone with whom I could vent all my feelings and not feel guilty. The longer the run, the more I vented. Sharing feelings about our screaming child with my wife just felt selfish. I justified my running as therapy and rationalized that I was far more stable at home as long as I had the frequent breaks away.

Our first 5K was right near my house. In telling Victoria which race we were doing, she questioned, "Why are you paying to run through the neighborhood you can run through for free?" I tried to rationally explain, "There's a goal to accomplish here *and* we get a T-shirt," I joked.

Carolina and I both cried crossing that first 5K finish line. The visual of us at the finish line of that race must have been a sight for onlookers. We were the last of the runners and the first of the walkers to cross the finish line—strollers with babies and dogs on leashes finished before we did.

But we didn't care—we weren't out to prove anything to anyone else. We shed tears of pure joy. We shrieked crossing the line, fists up in the air like Rocky Balboa, as though we just won an Olympic gold medal. We had completed our first race.

Fast-forward through several seasons of intense training and we found ourselves at the starting line of our first half marathon in fall 2014. We hadn't calculated into training that evening storms in Florida were common, so we went thinking we'd have great weather. The reality is that we were greeted at the starting line with a torrential downpour. We had *not* trained for this!

It took us just shy of three and a half hours because, as first-time Disney runners, we stopped to take pictures at every mile marker and we went to the bathroom several times. On one pit stop in Animal Kingdom, we rang out our shirts under the blow dryer only to get soaked again the moment we left the bathroom. Our feet were raw and blistered. It was raining buckets the entire way through; it didn't let up for a single moment. At one point during the race, there was a person with a megaphone atop a lifeguard chair in a parking lot shouting, "Watch out for the puddle!" We heard her after our feet were submerged ankle deep. We thought, "If we could finish this, we could do anything!" We felt like warriors!

You would imagine that if we cried, whooped, and hollered at the finish of our first 5K we would have gone nuts at the first half marathon finish. But no. We were really so miserable that we just wanted to be dry! It was so anticlimactic.

The following year, gluttons for punishment, seeking redemption, we went back to Disney World. However, this race was soon dubbed the "The Splash and Dash." Not Again!? Before the race even began, there were tornado warnings that prompted us (and 10,000+ fellow runners also looking for redemption from the year before) to funnel into the baseball stadium at the ESPN Wide World of Sports complex to be protected from the incoming storm. This seemed to be just more messages from the Universe that I was meant to keep overcoming challenges. And overcome I did.

Since childhood, I've always loved being outside. In the spring, summer, and fall, if I could stand the temperature, I might sleep outside on the deck to avoid listening to Alyssa's nonstop screaming. I would focus on nature, looking at the endless sky. This was in stark contrast to being indoors, where no matter what I did I couldn't drown out the sounds. Some nights, it was pure guttural incoherent screaming. Other nights, it was the sound of her voice repeating the same thing on a loop. She would scream, "I'm hungry!" at 4 a.m. every 10 seconds. With each passing time I heard the phrase, I could feel my blood pressure escalating. I would hide my head under my pillow. I would try hiding my head under both my pillow and Victoria's to no avail. I would put headphones on and crank up the volume of my music and I could still hear her screaming. It was intermittent, but any lull in the song would snap me immediately back into the present and the feelings of overwhelm would engulf me.

On a crisp, beautiful fall Saturday, I could get up and be out of the house before 8 a.m. Alyssa would already be awake and yelling since 6 a.m. I'd say, "I have a training run to do," validating my exit from the house. I'd run for hours.

I vividly remember being out on my morning runs crisscrossing over the train tracks that run near my house thinking, "I could end it all and make it look like an accident. The worst that can happen is that I kill myself." If I were to jack up the volume in my headphones and mindlessly (read: intentionally) run on to the tracks as the Amtrak is rolling on through, then it would look like an accident.

There were times I would run up my driveway at the end of a run and hear Alyssa screaming inside and run right back down the driveway and keep on going. There were times I was supposed to be doing a 3-mile run that turned into a 7-mile run—just because I couldn't deal with what was waiting for me at home. With Sia's "House on Fire" blaring in my ears I couldn't walk back into my figurative house on fire. By this point, I was so shut down emotionally that the thought of entering my home felt insurmountable.

Alyssa had the lungs of an opera singer. She had stamina. I felt like my running was to gather my breath and get more stamina and strength to deal with her. Admittedly, every time I left the house it was not without a tremendous amount of guilt. Every time I walked out that door, I knew I was subjecting Victoria to being alone with Alyssa while also managing Jackson.. I did this often and it wasn't fair to my wife, but if I didn't run, I may not have survived, which also would not have been fair to her. Nor would it have been fair to the kids because the person I would have become if I didn't have this outlet would not have been a pleasant mom to be around. We fought so hard to build this life and wanted this life, and now, I wanted nothing more than to run as far away as I could.

As a special education teacher, Victoria is professionally trained on how to ignore a litany of atypical behaviors. Victoria could sit in a room, watching TV, doing something on her phone, or reading while World War III levels of screaming surrounded her—all without being phased. Meanwhile, I'd be sitting in the same room as her, listening to Alyssa screaming nonstop, with adrenaline coursing through my bloodstream demanding every part of my body take action to get away.

My social media feeds are loaded with pictures of Jackson playing in the Home Depot shower displays or at Sears with an assortment of tools. Why? Because he and I were trying to escape. I would bring him anywhere to keep him occupied and away from the screaming—even if it was for only a few hours. One day in late January, we drove around decked out head to toe in St. Patrick's Day garb and then walked through the mall like that! Why? Just because.

While I would be pacing around our townhouse like a caged animal, crawling out of my skin, Jackson didn't realize that going shopping was a way to escape. To him, going shopping was just what we did on weekends. We'd go out and have fun. We'd go to the park. We'd visit friends. We'd visit grandparents. We'd go to the mall. For me, I had to leave or go mad. Victoria had empathy for me. She knew I was losing it—she could see it. As she endured the brunt of the screaming at home on her own, she would say, "Just take him with you."

My reservoir for handling Alyssa alone was minimal. Victoria could be alone with her for two days ignoring all her terrible behaviors. I, on the other hand, could not handle it for more than an hour. I tried. I really tried. Despite my best efforts, I just couldn't do it.

There were times when Alyssa would deliberately do something to get a reaction out of me and I would scream in response. But it didn't do any good; she did not stop or back down. I am not a screamer by nature. I don't raise my voice often. Living under that level of taunting, my discomfort would gather steam like a kettle about to boil. Alyssa would just sit there with this look that was not quite a smirk, but a look that made you question your own sanity. Deliberate. Intentional. Hurtful. She was fully aware of what she was doing. If I had asked her what she was thinking, it probably would have been, "I've got you where I want you." And, no doubt, this was bringing subconscious memories of my sister doing the exact same thing to me when we were growing up. That taunting look triggered a visceral reaction in my body. It brought back the horrible day when I lost control on my sister and pushed her literally up the wall by her neck. I did *not* want to be that kind of mother.

There were a handful of times when Victoria would go out with Jackson and I would be left alone with Alyssa. I would be hyperventilating when Victoria returned. Physically shaking. Unable to fully see straight. It was this crazy, crawling-out-of-my-skin feeling, like what I imagine the withdrawal from heroin might be. Small amounts of caffeine make me shaky, so I choose not to drink it—something I can control. Alyssa causes me to feel shaky and this is something I can't control—I have no recourse to get the shaking to stop.

Summer had always been hell on earth in my home due to lack of school-based structure and activities. Victoria taught summer school from 8 a.m. to 12 p.m. every day. There was an incident one day (there were probably many others, but I was too disassociated to remember) where I called Victoria crying, "You need to get home now!" I was sitting at the top of the stairs, sobbing. "If you don't come home now, I'm calling 211 and having myself taken away." Those were her two options. She came home immediately. I am not a crier. For me to be crying when I called her, she knew it was dire.

I said, "I can't do this. I am going to kill myself." I didn't fully mean those words, but I was at my breaking point (once again). If I called 211, which in addition to other things, is a psychiatric mobile crisis hotline intended to intervene on behalf of those in crisis, I would have begged for them to take me away. I believed I was saving Alyssa's life by getting myself out of the picture. But at the same time, I had the guilt of knowing I'd be endangering Victoria and Jackson's lives while trying to save my own if I had removed myself from the equation.

Meanwhile, I felt remorse for how I was ruining Victoria's life because she was more often than not stuck at home with Alyssa. I didn't act on any of the drastic things I was thinking because I didn't want to leave Victoria stranded. My love for Victoria stopped me from doing harm to myself. No one else was ever in danger; my irrational thoughts were squarely pointed inward.

Victoria, working with challenging children, observed how useless the 211 hotline was with other families in crisis. Understanding the system and knowing the pointlessness of calling 211 turned out to be detrimental to our ability to get Alyssa the help she needed later. We didn't have a laundry list of frantic 211 phone calls over an extended period of time, like many in our situation often do, because we knew how useless the responders would be when they showed up. The 211 service is not useless on a broad level, but it wasn't made for children with Alyssa's specific diagnosis.

Up to this point, our being well-educated was a benefit, as we were able to navigate the foster care system, adoption, and legal systems. But as we began to seek additional mental health support, we didn't have enough documentation when we requested a neuropsychological evaluation (an assessment of the brain). The results of a test like this would help us further understand the inner works of Alyssa's brain and what treatment plans would be more apt to work with her brain chemistry.

In 2012, when Alyssa was six, we began our search for answers and helpful information with her pediatrician. We asked her to give us a referral for the neuropsychological evaluation. She actually laughed directly in my face and dismissed my request. She questioned how we could possibly need such an extensive battery of testing. When Alyssa was in her office, she was an angel. "What could possibly be wrong with her?" the doctor thought. It must be us, the parents.

Despite laughing in my face (the ultimate kick you when you are in a down moment), the pediatrician reluctantly referred us to a child psychiatrist, Lisa, who was part of the same medical practice. At age six, Alyssa began seeing a psychiatrist and it was here, after some baseline psychological testing, we learned that she had Reactive Attachment Disorder (RAD). Various mental health resources used to diagnose psychiatric conditions—including the *Diagnostic and Statistical Manual, 5th Edition (DSM-5)*—describe reactive attachment disorder as:

> *[A] trauma- and stressor-related condition of early childhood caused by social neglect and maltreatment. Affected children have difficulty forming emotional attachments to others, show a decreased ability to experience positive emotion, cannot seek or accept physical or emotional closeness, and may react violently*

when held, cuddled, or comforted. Behaviorally, affected chil-
dren are unpredictable, difficult to console, and difficult to
discipline. Moods fluctuate erratically, and children may seem
to live in a "flight, fight, or freeze" mode. Most have a strong
desire to control their environment and make their own deci-
sions. Changes in routine, attempts to control, or unsolicited
invitations to comfort may elicit rage, violence, or self-injurious
behavior. In the classroom, these challenges inhibit the acquisi-
tion of core academic skills and lead to rejection from teachers
and peers alike.[1]

Parenting children with mental health challenges is a struggle unto itself. Societal stigma is ever present, and thus, every single day we must consciously and proactively choose to fight for our children, for our families, even on days where getting out and running away would be preferred.

With Reactive Attachment Disorder, children seek attention and behave unbearably to get it. If clinicians from 211 showed up, it would give Alyssa even more reason to behave horribly around us. Then, of course, while the 211 people were at the house, Alyssa would act like an angel. Once again, we would be looked upon as crazy and/or as bad parents—and she would be the misunderstood angel. This was a pattern we experienced over and over and over again in front of friends, family, and in every venue, mostly in school and anywhere public. We were being gaslighted by a six-year-old.

Inexplicably—despite my confidence in business—for some reason in my personal life, I doubted myself and listened to the external voices when it

---

[1] Ellis, Elizabeth E. and Abdolreza Saadabadi. "Reactive Attachment Disorder." Treasure Island, FL: StatPearls Publishing, 2020. https://www.ncbi.nlm.nih.gov/books/NBK537155/

came to child-rearing, something I feel many people can relate to. Through all of the experiences with Victoria and the children, there were many instances where, no, I didn't agree with what Victoria said or how she may have handled some situations, but ultimately, she was my ride-or-die. She was the one in the trenches with me, struggling to survive, to stay above water. I didn't have to worry about her judging me or vice versa. I consciously chose my wife over my mother (and others) so many times. She and I had to stick together, I resolved. We needed to be a united front. So, when the incident happened at Alyssa's seventh birthday over a stupid piece of cake, it was blown way out of proportion in my mind and I exploded. I had hit yet another breaking point.

My one culinary skillset is cake decorating. I spent so much time baking and then decorating the perfect Hello Kitty birthday cake because that's what Alyssa wanted.

Due to my mother's ever-intensifying Parkinson's disease, she couldn't drive to Connecticut from Rhode Island alone, and asked her friend, June, to come with her and drive. It was mid-November and my mom entered the house outfitted in typical "Kathleen fashion," which was a combination of stained clothing and unsavory smells. This wasn't new, but I was embarrassed more than usual. This was what I knew my whole life. I was used to making excuses—and distancing myself and disassociating during these events.

Victoria's parents arrived for the birthday party. Linda, Victoria's mother, had her hair done and, as usual, was dressed stylishly and looked healthy, vibrant. Linda and my mom were around the same age, but side by side, there was no comparison. My mom aged visibly fast for her age. June also looked fashionable.

I thought of my mom, compared her to Maria. I looked at Victoria's put-together parents and I was bitten by the envy bug. I asked myself, why couldn't I have even a glimpse of that in my life? A hint of stability, anything resembling a vision of "normalcy?"

What I noticed was that Victoria's family had empathy toward my mother. Empathy I don't think I was able to conjure at the time. I could see that others genuinely felt for sorry my mom because her health was always bad, since the time I was 14. It is ironic that my mother was a nurse and spent so much time healing others but had so many issues herself and no one there to help heal her.

The real me functioned behind this façade that *I* am a well put together human and yet, when someone sees me with my family, I think I am exposed as a fraud as one glimpses from whence I came. I felt shame, a familiar emotion. And all of this was running through my head as I prayed that my daughter would make it through the whole party without melting down into screaming hysterics.

After we blew out the candles and sang happy birthday and everyone had their piece of cake, my mother came at me when I stopped her from handing my daughter a second piece of cake. My mother didn't understand (or hear about) the havoc my daughter would cause in our home if she ate all that sugar after being on best behavior all day. My mother didn't care that our home would be intolerable for 36 hours because of an additional Hello Kitty sliver. My mother with her watery, blank eyes just wanted to treat her granddaughter and became hostile with me for stopping her.

Persistent questioning of our house rules by outsiders is so upsetting to me. The truth was that Alyssa was lucky she was able to have even *one* piece of cake, considering the hell she put us through prior to the party. She was lucky we didn't just cancel the party altogether—which was strongly considered only hours before anyone showed up at our door.

Trying to explain the cake situation to my mother, who should know better having raised Amanda, was futile. My mom was not in a rational thought mode and no matter what I would say she was not going to understand.

The odd thing was, it was my mom who was pushing for Alyssa to have the second piece. Alyssa hadn't asked aloud for another piece. Alyssa was playing the angel role and not saying a word, looking so sadly at my mother because she couldn't have more cake. She was giving Grammy puppy dog eyes. Though her eyes actually were focused on me and Victoria, challenging us. No one else would notice it, because they weren't trained to look for it. Victoria and I were professionals at recognizing Alyssa's manipulation. I could almost hear my daughter thinking, "Go ahead, Mom. Tell Grammy why you won't let me have more cake. I want more cake and Grammy is going to give it to me!"

The whole cake thing wasn't a huge scene, but more of a pissing match between my mother and me. Fortunately, not everyone witnessed this exchange. The end result was hearing what lousy parents we were and how we were doing it all wrong. Did she actually believe she had done everything perfectly? I begged to differ.

After so many incidents, years of feeling unsupported, unappreciated, judged, and lectured to by my mother (and other family members), we didn't have room in our home or hearts for anything but positivity. I just could not allow the negativity of my mother to keep sending me into self-doubt and depressive spirals. This was the proverbial straw that broke the camel's back. I made the dramatic and conscious decision on this "cake day" to cut my mother out of my life—and my children's—completely.

Age 33

In the summer of 2014, Victoria and I were invited to her closest friend's wedding in New Jersey. It was scheduled during our annual *how to vacation and yet avoid hotels at all costs* camping trip, so we decided to combine the two events and chose a camping site in New Jersey. At this point, I had already believed I had hit rock bottom, but it was a false door, there was still plenty more to drop.

This particular camping trip was the worst on record. Alyssa was behaving more wretchedly than she ever had before. In addition to her screaming, as she got older, she began to get violent—throwing things, deliberately breaking things, and being outright indignant. She wouldn't walk when she was supposed to walk or go where we all wanted to go. This was more than typical childish stubborn behavior.

As we usually do, we had picked the most remote campsite we could out of respect for other campers. Our criteria for picking a campground was always a two-bedroom deluxe cabin with full plumbing—which would allow for Alyssa to have her own bedroom to scream in and we would have a kitchenette to cook Jackson meals, since his food anxieties manifested in incredible pickiness.

On the day of the wedding, we had to pick ourselves up during this camping nightmare and get ready to go to a wedding. We had no idea what kind of behavior we were going to see out of Alyssa when we got to the reception hall.

In typical fashion, Alyssa was the star of the show. People commented on how sweet she was—how demure she was—and just so damn cute! This was yet another breaking point that had us realizing what an untenable situation we were in. We could not win.

For the most part, our daughter's horrible behaviors were confined to *just* the three of us seeing them. So, when we'd explain what was happening at home to someone and then they'd see our tiny, pretty, delicate flower of a child out with us, their brains couldn't compute how we could be describing the same child. This is a big component of RAD. The closer and safer someone becomes to a child with RAD, the more intensely the child wants to destroy that relationship.

Alyssa was a charming angel with strangers because strangers weren't a threat—strangers didn't know her. She could manipulate strangers into getting what she wanted, whereas she couldn't with us. Around this time, Victoria's parents really started to understand what we were going through, which was a relief. They were the only people we trusted to be alone with Alyssa. But it is purely because Victoria's parents were getting closer and closer to Alyssa and her RAD brain was telling her she had to fight her grandparents away too.

In the short time we were out at the wedding and reception, all was quiet on the Alyssa front because she was among strangers. But the moment we got back to the campground our terror situation escalated dramatically. Alyssa's intensity was higher because she ate more than usual and had sugar-laden treats at the wedding. It's harder to follow our usual sugar restriction policies when at a function where we can't control what is served and have less ability to monitor what Alyssa can find to consume. By the end of this camping trip, we recognized that this was the worst Alyssa had ever been and made the disappointing decision that it was to be our last family camping trip.

Age 34

In July of 2015, Maria was having her annual backyard party for her birthday. She and I had originally met when she was looking for landscaping for this same annual event, 16 years before.

Maria, at first, didn't really believe what Victoria and I were going through with Alyssa's behaviors—that is until we all tried camping together. The four of us, years before that final camping trip, had joined Maria and her husband Gary, her brother, his wife, and their two kids, at a campsite. We stayed in a combination of cabins and tents. And, as was typical, Alyssa screamed for hours on end in one of the cabins. Maria went into the cabin believing she was going to be the Alyssa Whisperer. She was in the cabin alone with Alyssa and the screaming stopped. Victoria and I looked at each other, eyebrows raised. Wow! Impressive. And then it started again. Victoria and I nodded at each other. "Yeah, that makes sense."

Maria had gone in with an "I can fix it" confidence (apple doesn't fall far from the tree?) and came out shortly thereafter completely defeated. During this particular incident Maria got more than a glimpse into what Victoria and I were dealing with every day, year after year. I believe the overwhelm of our situation finally clicked for Maria. She was frustrated in one afternoon and we were dealing with this every single day and most nights too.

This one microcosm of our home experience during the camping trip provided external validation that what we were saying we were experiencing at home was accurate to our family. But I didn't say anything to Maria. The mere fact that she had experienced Alyssa's tirade of tears and yelling was enough for us to believe we may have found an ally who understood the depth and complexity of our home life. Up to this point, our entire world was filled with judgment from people who just couldn't "get it" and, sadly, many chose not to try.

Several years after this coming-to-awareness camping trip, I hired Maria to come work for me as an administrative assistant. We worked together for about two years. We talked daily, a mix of personal and professional stuff. It was an amazing experience—while it lasted. During these two years, Maria had an up-close view of what was really going on in my life and house because, at any point when we were on the phone and I was working from home, she could hear the screaming in the background. Or I would be debriefing her on the latest events.

So, when Jackson and I were coming alone to the annual backyard party, my birth mother understood on a deeper level what must have been happening at home. She had a different vantage point than many others in our life at the time. I believe she was consciously trying to fully understand our situation.

Jackson and I left home the morning of the party expecting to have a great time with family. He was so excited to spend time in the pool with his great uncles and his cousins. We arrived and I joined all the adults on a crowded deck talking and supervising the action in the pool. Jackson went off to swim with his cousins.

Maria's mother (my birth grandmother), whom I didn't see often, was there from Arizona. She and Maria were in the house with some family members, while I was sitting outside with all my aunts, four of them in total. We were relishing catching up since it's not often that we we're all together.

I could observe Jackson in the pool playing (he could stay in water all day) with family. Out of nowhere, Maria's husband Gary walked militantly around the corner, came toward the table where I was sitting and just unleashed!

Gary started screaming at me, telling me what a "shit mother" I am—that Victoria and I are bad parents. He went on to say how I favor Jackson and how Alyssa is treated like trash and is never allowed out of the house. I stood there, jaw agape, for his full two minutes of unfiltered rage directed at me, while my aunts sat in shock. And, just as suddenly as it started, it was like a switch was hit, it ended. We all just sat stunned, staring at Gary's back as he stomped off the way he had come. I made eye contact with my aunts. None of us knew what to say. We were all thinking, "What just happened?"

While fighting back tears, I took this assault as my cue to leave. If I wasn't wanted there, I was certainly not going to stay. No one in the house or in the pool had any idea of what had transpired on the deck outside. Why do people feel they know best how to raise other people's children? No two children are exactly alike and what works for you and yours doesn't work for everyone else. This is magnified when you are parenting a child with severe mental health needs.

I calmed my heart rate so I could talk without the hostility bubbling inside me and casually announced that we were going to hit the road. Maria insisted on a family photo before we left. I fake smiled, while sobbing on the inside.

When I started packing Jackson up to leave, he was disappointed and upset because he was having a good time and did not understand why we had to go. Jackson had expected that we were going to spend the night, as that was the plan we packed for and discussed.

Just as I was about to pull away, Gary came around from behind the house, reeking of marijuana, and tried to apologize. I dismissed him and drove away.

I couldn't wrap my head around how Gary had come up with this line of verbal abuse. Why did he think voicing his thoughts in a tirade in front of half my family was the ideal way to communicate? He dug a knife into my heart in a cruel, cruel way. Internally, I was already spiraling to my rock bottom, despite what my external appearances may have shown to the world around me. Gary hit me when I was down. To have someone throw judgment at me when he really didn't know the situation we were in, was really hard to handle.

All of these attacks against our parenting style came when the deliverers were operating with limited facts. Rather than ask, "How can we help?" or "How can we support you?" Gary, for example, chose the path of a judgmental rant versus lending a hand to family members in need.

Logically, I worked out in my head on the ride home from that party that it might have been something Maria had commented on at some point; maybe while venting her frustration at being unable to solve my problems for me. At the time, I didn't believe Maria agreed with anything Gary threw at me.

When I got home, I sent Maria a text, in a very direct (albeit dramatic) manner, that basically said: *What Gary did to me today is unforgivable; I will never forgive him. His relationship is dead to me.*

Maria texted back immediately: *OMG! What happened?*

It was then that I realized she didn't even know what had transpired earlier in the day. Gary and her sisters never told her.

She then texted: *I'm sorry.*

I never blamed Maria for the incident and I was able to separate her from her husband, but she wasn't able to do the same.

From that event in July until the end of December, Maria and I continued to work together, but it was awkward. We kept our interactions strictly on email and no longer spoke on the phone personally or professionally like we once did daily. Somehow, we were able to get things done without our strained relationship impacting anyone around us. After months of building tension, that January Maria made it clear that she was done working with me professionally and communicating with me personally. To this day, she has never asked for my side of the story of what happened. It hurts that she didn't care enough about me—her child—to try to even talk to me. She didn't reach out or express how she felt so we could talk it through. Her sisters may have told her the chronology of what happened, but she never checked in on me to get my interpretation of what it felt like. In that moment, Maria chose Gary over me. He's still in her life, and I'm not. Whatever Gary felt at the party that set him off must have been more important than her relationship with me, and that hurts. The fact that I still don't know what caused Gary's outburst makes our separation even more bewildering. It was a miracle to find Maria and have her in my life, and this loss still saddens me beyond words.

Victoria and I didn't know why so many people felt they had the right to judge us. Not even just judge us privately, but out in the open, publicly witnessed, directly to our faces. No one knew the details of what was happening at home nor cared enough to ask. If we weren't physically or mentally abusing our children in front of them, what (or who) gives anyone else the right to pass judgment on how we parent our children? This is a common struggle for parents with perfectly typical functioning children. But when we are talking about children with special needs, there is a heightened need for sensitivity.

Hearing my mother's voice with all its judgmental harshness could be a trigger in ways I wasn't able to unpack at the time. I think specific language may have been used that was echoing things my mother and/or sister may have said while I was growing up. Hearing that language directed at me and Victoria triggered an emotional response of a child being hurt by a parent. Psychologists would say that I don't want to be thought of as my mother. I don't want to be thought of as hurting my kids the way my mother or sister hurt me.

Part of Reactive Attachment Disorder is the ability to triangulate adults against each other. Triangulation is a manipulative tactic to engineer rivalry between two people. My daughter was constantly setting up a divide and conquer scenario between other people where she would come out the winner. She was the queen of playing one person against another. It is a gift. It was a survival mechanism for her as a young child. Victoria and I were always the losers of this game.

Amanda did the same thing when we were growing up. I know what this game looks like. And there I was—playing it again.

PART VII

DESTRUCTION

Ages: 34-36

October 2015-June 2017

Age 34

At the risk of sounding like a crazy cat lady (who am I kidding? *I am* a crazy cat lady), I firmly believe my soul mate was a handsome gray tabby cat named Remy. My entire life I have always had a cat and never did one of them occupy a place in my heart and soul as Remy did. Remy entered my life back in 2004, when Jamie and I were dating and she thought he would make a great birthday gift for me.

One day, late in 2015 Remy suddenly became lethargic. Even though he was my office mate and sat with me much of my workday, I hadn't noticed his declining health. I don't know if I didn't want to see it or if I was blinded by my adrenaline from being in constant fight or flight mode with Alyssa. Remy was only 11 and I foolishly didn't think there was anything wrong with him. I had expected him to live until he turned 20, like the two grumpy calico cats I grew up with.

One night, Victoria and I were sitting on the couch and I casually commented, half asking, "Why is Remy so lethargic?" And she, in the most cold and heartless way, said, "It's because he's dying!" It was a knock-the-wind-out-of-you kind of punch to the gut. I couldn't believe this was her reaction. Her words and attitude were so hurtful. I truly don't think she intended it to sound as horrible as it came out. The gravity of the potential of losing my soul mate before he reached 20 was not something my fried brain was able to compute. Hysterics were my only reaction.

The next day, my first order of business was to take Remy to the vet to see if anything was actually wrong. After a battery of tests, I received the worst news possible—my prince had kidney disease. My visions of Remy living to 20 years hastily shortened to maybe he'll live six months. My world was shattered at this diagnosis. Through all the baggage of ex-girlfriends and child-related drama, he was my constant companion. If I needed to cry, I would cry in his fur to muffle the sound. If I landed a new client, I would pick him up and twirl him while singing some victory song. He was always there for me.

Within a few short months, he began losing a lot of weight. Rescued from a barn in the backwoods of Connecticut, legend had it that Remy's mother had been impregnated by a bobcat (whether or not that was even biologically possible). He was a 15-pound cat with a bobcat face and not an ounce of fat. We knew he wasn't a typical domestic cat but were unsure of what kind of cat that actually made him. He had wild beastly tendencies.

Remy had always been overaggressive. He hated people. He used to walk on the counters or tables when the kids would be eating and he would just smack the food right out of their hands and walk off. If you've ever seen an episode of *My Cat from Hell*, then you know the type. Admittedly, he could be difficult, but he was my baby and cuddled and spooned with me every night in bed.

In spring 2016, I had gone to California for a client training. Victoria called while I was driving my rental car back from a meeting. Through the Bluetooth in my ear, my wife said quite seriously, "I have something to tell you." In my head I'm thinking, what happened? Who's sick? Is the house still standing? Victoria said that Sue (her best friend) didn't think she should tell me right now because there was nothing I could do, but Victoria knew I wouldn't forgive her if she didn't tell me something I needed to hear.

"What is it Victoria? Just spit it out!" I said dreading what I was about to hear.

"I don't think Remy is going to make it through the night," she solemnly shared, like someone had already died.

"Oh, fuck," escaped from my mouth. "My flight home is tomorrow morning. I'll be home within 24 hours." I told my wife. But I worried, would I make it before Remy passed?

I sobbed relentlessly and messily with tissues all over the rental car, hotel room, cab to the airport, and on my flight. I flew cross-country all of the following day. I wore dark sunglasses to hide my blotchy face and random coin-sized tears. I was definitely giving off a do-not-talk-to-me vibe. My travel style was Unabomber-chic—with my hoodie up, sunglasses on, slouched down in my seat, arms crossed around my chest, and leg vibrating with impatience to get there already! Years later, I found myself in the same situation flying across the country trying to make it to my mom's side before she passed.

When I walked into the house, Victoria approached me like I might set off a bomb if she moved too quickly. She was trying to explain to me what had happened and why Remy was in trouble; why she was so worried. "Remy was still alive!" was all I could process at first.

The story started to come out. Remy had retreated to behind the toilet of our master bath. Victoria and I went over and over what could have happened early Thursday evening that would have caused this. Victoria believed that Alyssa kicked Remy, who was sitting on the landing at the top of the stairs, while on the way to take a shower. Remy hadn't come out of the bathroom since, Victoria shared.

As I entered the bathroom, I could see Remy was traumatized. I reached out to him and he retreated farther behind the toilet. He wouldn't come out despite my coaxing. He and I had a soul connection on a deep indescribable level and for him to retreat from me was foreign. Eventually, after a few days, as long as I stayed in our bedroom Remy was as lovable as usual, hopped up on my lap and cuddled for as long as I could sit still. If I left the bedroom, he raced back into the bathroom and went behind the toilet. I spent from the end of March until the end of April working on my laptop from the bathroom floor, coaxing and cajoling to get Remy to come out.

As disturbing as the new behavior was, the more frightening issue was that Remy had ripped out two inches of fur on the back of his neck. He had pulled hair out until it was down to a disgusting 2-inch blister.

Something was not adding up. Remy was my office mate. For the better part of his life, I worked from home and he had been my copilot, taking up residence on my desk or sitting in his makeshift bed by my feet.

I called my friend Diana, a hospice nurse and animal lover. She soothed me and gently suggested, "Maybe Remy's trying to tell you it's his time to go?"

I asked Victoria to call the vet about in-home euthanasia options for when we would be ready. This was a call I could not make. Victoria called, explained the situation, and the vet asked us to bring Remy in again.

I brought Remy to the vet. I explained everything, how this is not how he normally behaves but I was not sure if he was actually dying or about to go. She told me that, based on everything I said, she firmly believed something traumatic happened to him. The vet gave me examples of other animals who had behaved similarly. She thought Remy could have somehow been scratched or cut, which would have provoked him to pull all of his fur out in that area to soothe it.

The vet wasn't sure if Remy would ever want to leave my room again but told me to just meet him where he is and know that his kidneys are not in complete failure yet, but that he needs space because something had traumatized him.

Something made me ask the vet, dreading the answer, "Could my daughter have kicked him?" Internally, I wondered to myself, "Would Alyssa have kicked Remy?" I answered myself, "Of course she could kick him." I started to think she could actually have done something to him. Which led to many guilty feelings over did she or didn't she and how could I think that of my child?

I went back in my mind, replaying what I knew, as I drove home from the vet's office. Victoria was home alone with both kids. Alyssa had had a limited unsupervised window of time on the night of the incident, the beginning of Remy's fear, so it seemed plausible that during that time she may have done something to him. Previously, we had been thinking even if he were kicked or thrown it wouldn't cause this type of scared reaction, so we passed it off, but the vet confirmed otherwise.

The bottom line was that it looked quite likely that my daughter harmed my Prince Charming in some way that caused the traumatic reaction. Knowing my daughter's history and her mental health diagnosis, animal cruelty is sadly on the top of the list of behaviors we might see. With the strict routine and structure we had put in place in the house, we went out of our way to ensure Alyssa would never have access to animals alone.

Victoria and I decided not to ask Alyssa about the incident because if it was an accident (i.e., she picked him up, he scratched her, and she threw him into something), then we didn't want to plant the seed in her mind for future ways to get attention, which could include harming animals. We also didn't want her carrying this guilt (if she was even capable of feeling guilt) if that wasn't what had happened and she genuinely had nothing to do with it.

In the end, when it was Remy's time, Victoria called the mobile vet who specialized in euthanizing animals in the most humane way at home with family. The vet gave Remy an injection. Remy was resting on an old University of North Carolina light blue hooded sweatshirt, on my work desk, with me holding his head in my hands and looking into his dark, mysteriously beautiful eyes. I was trying to send love energy his way through my tears and he looked back at me. I could almost hear him say, "Thank you, Mom." On my desk is where Remy wanted to die—which was very fitting.

For me, this was the worst experience in recent memory and I felt like I went through it alone. My family doesn't handle death well. I was dramatic, inconsolable, leading up to and on the day of Remy's passing and that didn't help. I believe Victoria did her best and opted to give me space because no matter what she did or didn't do in that time, it wasn't what I felt I needed. I don't know if Remy would have lived much longer based on his previous kidney diagnosis, but this was a sad way to go out—scared and traumatized.

The following morning, I woke up to the sound of a phantom meow coming from the bathroom that echoed through my bedroom. I woke forgetting he had passed, but when I remembered, I took that as a sign that he was telling me he was okay.

I don't know, nor will I ever know, what really happened. I believe Alyssa was genuinely upset when Remy died. She didn't seem remorseful or guilty, hiding a secret, or anything like that, but she is incapable of expressing emotion mostly—unless it's raging and screaming. Jackson was really upset for a while, but he fell in love with Leena (Remy's doppelganger, whom we adopted from the shelter a few weeks after Remy passed) and he would pick her up for comfort. I was a train wreck for a very long time after losing Remy. He was my baby—my soul—my world.

I feel like this incident with Remy was not helping my frame of mind around safety in our house. If Alyssa had this millisecond window of opportunity where she was unguarded, unsupervised, and this is what happened, what would happen with me or Jackson in the future? Wouldn't things just get worse as Alyssa got older, taller, stronger? Wasn't her birth mother, my sister, capable of burning down our childhood home?

I don't believe Alyssa would have tried to go after Victoria because Victoria is generally stronger. I was the weak one in the herd and my daughter knew it. I believed her instinct would be to come after me. There is a specific look one gets in their eyes when they are cooking up something of an evil nature. I had seen this look many times prior and tried to avoid it and ignore it. After the Remy experience, I had no doubt that something *could* happen. My instincts kicked me into self-preservation mode.

I started to have dreams that Alyssa would stab me to death, in the same ways I thought Amanda would kill me growing up. I couldn't sleep. I was haunted with horrible scenarios playing out in my mind the minute I closed my eyes—and the mere sound of my own daughter's voice could send my body into a paralyzing anxiety state.

During school, Alyssa manipulated everyone around her. This was a byproduct of simple math—one teacher, 20 students. Teachers can't dedicate all their attention to one child's behaviors. So, despite the Individualized Education Plan (IEP) which was a legal document showing all of her teachers and those around her how her behaviors should be addressed—we know they weren't always following the plan and that her behaviors were not necessarily being dealt with appropriately. It became a game to Alyssa. How far could she push it? How much could she steal in one day before anyone caught on? How badly could she hurt another child and feign an accident before a teacher realized it was intentional?

Alyssa was so distracted by planning her next conquest/challenge/attack/theft that she was unable to pay attention. We got calls many times a week with status reports and complaints about Alyssa's behaviors. If she couldn't get attention through her deeds, she would slip into hypochondriac mode and we'd get calls about her latest physical ailment.

Most of the time, living with Alyssa was not pleasurable. Not for her. Not for us. The worse she got, the more it became like she was a prisoner in our house. Nobody wants to be a warden for their own child.

She would come in the front door after school, go up the stairs and into her room. An adult would walk behind her the whole way. She would throw a two-hour tantrum until we gave up trying to get her to complete her homework. Naturally, her grades suffered when we gave up homework duty.

Her door would be open most of the time, so we could see in. And there was nothing in the room that could be used as a weapon of any kind. We only shut her door and locked it when we absolutely had to during the day when she got really out of control. But we locked her in at night—for everyone's safety. We knew this wasn't "the right" thing to do, but it was anticipatory self-defense; it was the safe and necessary thing to do in our house.

She had a strict schedule for when she used the bathroom, ate, or played. We learned after many times of hearing her scream that she needed the bathroom, and then didn't go but instead used the time to destroy anything in her path, that we couldn't believe anything she said. A schedule would give her what she physically needed and still protect the rest of the family. Because reality was that the more time she had without restrictions, supervision, or boundaries, the worse the damage would be.

Alyssa looked to the world like a sweet harmless spirit. "How could someone so cute and so tiny scream the way you're saying?" people would ask—condescendingly, like there must be something wrong with us. Eventually, we became so paranoid that the police or CPS would show up on any day of the week, that we began documenting everything. This included audio, video, photographs, and handwritten notes. In the presence of a naysayer I would say, "I have an audio recording. Would you like me to play it?" And when I pressed play and Alyssa's performance began, you could see these judger's eyes glaze over. I wish we had started sharing this kind of information earlier, but we were embarrassed and closeted about the whole situation. We didn't want people really seeing or hearing the reality of what we lived with, but it was only by doing so that we began to become free.

We had security cameras installed in her room from two angles. The images were grainy and blurry, but enough for us to see if she was potentially in danger. I felt no guilt showing a 30-second clip of Alyssa naked, flailing around, hanging off of her doorknob like a gymnast or pounding on her bedroom windows to someone who believed I was lying or making all of this up. However, when they visibly saw the evidence, they would shrink away and stop talking. There was nothing more to say. If you had help to offer, we were truly open to constructive suggestions! "Otherwise," I would say in my head, "keep your opinions to yourself! If you haven't lived it, you can't possibly know or understand."

There were times we filmed incidents with our phones. When we pressed *record* during an extreme situation, Alyssa would change her screaming to something different the second the camera was pointed toward her.

She would yell things such as, "I want to go to the bathroom!" or she was too hot/cold, or she was *so* hungry. Therefore, if we tried to show someone, a person would have instant empathy and say, "Well, she had to use the bathroom," or "She clearly just wanted a sweater." This was never the case—she was playing all of us—skillfully. With the end goal of placing doubt in the minds of others, as to whether Victoria and I were fit to be parents.

We always had to keep the windows closed in our house because Alyssa's screaming was loud enough that the neighbors could hear (and still could even with the windows closed.) We began with installing soundproofing materials disguised as artwork, but it wasn't enough. Jackson was living in the house wearing noise-cancelling headphones meant for outdoor use like mowing a lawn or using a leaf blower to drown out his sister's never-ending screaming. The three of us would all have headphones on, individually doing whatever it took to survive, while Alyssa raged on. Then, in the next phase, we had to install child safety gadgets around the home to keep Alyssa from grabbing anything that could be used to hurt herself, us, her brother, or our cat; setting things on fire; or stealing things.

Alyssa took to screaming in her bedroom window with more intensity as neighbors passed by walking their dogs. At some point, we had to remove the curtains from her windows because they posed a danger to her. She could choke while trying to eat them, shred them, hang herself with them, light them on fire—so many options for malicious behavior from a simple set of curtains. Her efforts at getting attention from the neighbors worked—she had an audience as they would pass by with their dogs in tow.

We watched the monitors with the feed from the cameras to be sure Alyssa was safe but also, to be honest, to collect evidence to prove that it wasn't us beating her or doing any bodily harm. She was doing this to herself deliberately.

In between wanting to kill myself and wishing I could just run away, I cried as my heart was torn to pieces that I couldn't remove, change, or fix whatever was torturing my child into acting this way.

We purchased Victoria's childhood family home and thus Victoria had a long history on our street and had friendships with the majority of the neighbors nearby. This was a blessing. They knew enough to know that whatever they might be hearing from the outside is not what it might sound like is happening on the inside. If they were really concerned, they could knock on our door, come inside, and see for themselves. We had an open-door policy for anyone with a desire to understand.

One neighbor in particular walked around our block daily. As she passed by, she would intently stare at our house, almost as if it were haunted. From the outside, all she saw was a petite child screaming, staring back at her, and/or beating on her window.

Alyssa had developed an almost daily routine of standing in her window naked and screaming. Victoria and I had to do what we could to mitigate the situation. Victoria would stay inside to ensure Alyssa was safe while Jackson and I would go out to the front yard, play some catch, and then sit out in lawn chairs in our driveway. If anyone was walking by, nosy neighbors be damned, they could see mother and son outside acting normally, obviously not causing harm to the one screaming and banging from inside the house. Jackson had no idea that this is not normal. Just like I had no idea growing up that my sister's behaviors weren't normal.

I tried to reserve my distaste and anger toward the judgmental neighbor because I didn't know her. When she began gossiping and speculating to another neighbor about what she thought was happening in our home, she did not get the reaction she intended. What this nosy neighbor did not know is that Victoria knew the other woman she was gossiping to really well. Nosy stated, "Something's going on in there." And our friendly neighbor replied, "You have no idea what they're going through. There's no reason to call anyone." Had our ally neighbor not done that, we feel certain CPS and/or the local police department would have been at our doorstep earlier.

Meanwhile, our neighbor to the right worked for CPS. The one to the left was a Hartford police officer. The neighbor behind us was a local town police officer. Every day, I defended myself in my head with what I wanted to say to this nosy neighbor, "You don't think that if something was going to happen, they would have investigated us by now?"

Every single damn day, we lived in fear and worried that someone was going to show up and arrest us for child abuse. Fortunately, we had many professional allies—the psychiatrist, the therapist, the elementary school principal, the school psychologist, and the social worker. We knew any one of them would have our backs if we needed to defend ourselves. And we would need them all eventually.

When Victoria and I first started watching my niece and nephew on weekends, we knew we were falling in love with each other—and with children with some complicated challenges. As a special education teacher, she was confident that she could handle anything that was put in front of us and I loved and trusted her and all her confidence. If anyone could handle these children's special needs, we were sure it was us!

As the kids aged, each child's unique needs became clearer. Our son developed his own personality and we saw that he spent much of his time coping with his sister's behaviors. His food anxieties had become more pronounced.

Knowing my sister's history, we were not surprised that Alyssa was becoming more and more aggressive in her behaviors. That didn't make it any easier to manage or cope. We wanted help. We needed help. We were in a full-on struggle to survive. I remembered the tortured life I had dealing with my sister breaking into my room, constantly taunting me, creating havoc with my relationship with my parents. I didn't want that for my son.

There was no realistic way all our family members would stay alive if we tried to cohabitate for much longer. While that might sound dramatic, we realized there was no scenario in which we could keep Alyssa in our home.

A compounding factor in addressing our kids' mental health needs was the fact that, since they were adopted, they were eligible for the state health insurance program. The upside is that their insurance covered *everything*. The downside is that every doctor's visit or phone call we'd make, they'd assume, before we walked in the door, that we were low income, or possibly that *we* also had mental health needs and somehow (as unfair as it is) that changed how they responded to us.

Alyssa and I look enough alike that doctors initially assumed she's biologically my child. I continually had to inform the specialists, for the record, that I'm adopted, Alyssa is adopted. There's no blood relation. I had to remind them that her mental health needs were not a result of my genetics. We were judged all the time. I admit I was a tad defensive.

Sometimes, I wondered if we had not been on state insurance would we have been taken more seriously earlier on, rather than having to constantly prove ourselves to be worthy of care? Would doctors have been more responsive to testing? Would we have had access to more help—different help, better help?

Once we were in the room with any health professionals, they could see that Alyssa and Jackson's parents were two well-educated women. Specialists would quickly realize we weren't the stereotype they were expecting and they couldn't push us around. We had our binders of history and reports. We came prepared to find solutions. They also saw that they couldn't just ignore us, or merely pacify us, as they likely do with so many. They knew we were armed with data and ready to go toe to toe with them.

In these moments, I thought about all of the other parents going through similar situations and how much more of an uphill battle they were probably facing because they didn't know how to square off with mental health professionals the way we eventually were able to.

With the Reactive Attachment Disorder diagnosis, we hoped to get a treatment protocol for our daughter, but we got nothing.

Just months before the birthday cake fiasco, I called my mother to share information from the psychiatrist's report about RAD and, in response to what I told her, she casually said, "Oh, your sister had that." I thought I didn't hear her right—did she just casually mention this is something my sister, Alyssa's birth mother, dealt with in childhood? HEY, MOM, that genetic information would have been *really* helpful information to know years ago and could have impacted a course of treatment and changed our lives! *Frustrated* was only one of the emotions going through my brain at that moment.

It took us years before we found professionals who would give us the time of day, and then believe us when we described the issues we were running into. Had we had this valuable piece of family health information would we have understood what we were dealing with and been able to find the right help sooner? I believe my mom's reactions and lack of sharing relevant information reflected her naiveté about what to do with her own daughter during the time Amanda was growing up. My mother blocked things out, mostly through drinking. Writing from a place of healing, I can see that my mom, both of my parents, were doing the best they could, given the situation they were in with their adopted children. My mom was addicted to alcohol. I was addicted to running. Escape was the same goal either way.

Around this time, disagreements with Victoria became frequent. Unlike the fights my parents had over my mother's alcohol abuse, our disagreements never turned into screaming matches. But as a couple, we were at odds about our next steps. On parenting issues, though I didn't always agree, I deferred to my wife, the expert in the field. My father, when he left us, surrendered care of his girls to my mother, a nurse. As a result, I was starting to feel powerless again. It was easier to just go along. Agreeing was the only way to save myself, which had to be my primary goal—survival. The parallels to my youth were not clear to me while I was in the situation but have come to light as I've moved on.

We had tried taking Alyssa to multiple therapists, but nothing was working. We needed to find someone with attachment disorder expertise, which was hard to find in our area. Thankfully, we finally found Lorna, the right person, after hitting countless dead ends in the years prior. We lucked out that Lorna's office wasn't far from our house.

I started bringing Alyssa to sessions once a week on Tuesdays throughout 2015. Then we attended sessions twice weekly for all of 2016. Overall, I would say we had a good relationship with Lorna the whole time we worked with her. I was the one primarily managing the whole process. I took Alyssa to 99% of the appointments because I had the flexibility in my schedule to do so.

Talk therapy isn't known to work overly well with children with Reactive Attachment Disorder. It honestly didn't seem like the therapy was doing a whole lot of good for Alyssa, but Lorna was an attachment specialist and we were trusting the process. Visiting Lorna was worth the trip, even if it only helped me feel saner on a regular basis! There was value for both Alyssa and me in these twice weekly sessions. I had an outlet to say, "This is what Alyssa did this week," and thus got that off my chest.

For Lorna, I had a reason to streamline our documentation process at home even further. Having thorough documentation definitely benefited us as we began researching other avenues to get our daughter help.

Having Lorna as an advocate gave us emotional and mental support we weren't aware we needed. Lorna came to school with us several times for IEP meetings with the teaching team. She helped connect us to additional resources. She listened to our struggles and helped us understand how Alyssa processed and saw things. Alyssa's behavior wasn't changing or reducing in severity, but our family was gaining a better understanding of what we were dealing with, assurances that we weren't the cause of our daughter's behaviors, and we learned coping skills.

Age 35

Holidays and special occasions are always the worst with children with Reactive Attachment Disorder. Alyssa's behaviors got increasingly worse any time a holiday would roll around. I dreaded the holidays. I dreaded downtime and school vacation time. I dreaded days off. I dreaded snow days. Departure from routine and schedules of any kind would be triggers for a period of emotional and physical roller-coaster experiences.

On Christmas Eve 2015, our daughter flipped over her two bedroom dressers, hooked her feet around the dresser legs, and hung her body, face down, dangerously out the second-story window. I screamed in panic when I saw this. Victoria and I were able to haul her back in the window without injury.

As we set the dressers upright, we saw that Alyssa had been breaking pieces off the back of the dresser for an unknown purpose. Saving them for what? My mind went straight to the fire that consumed my childhood home. What was Alyssa planning?

In SWAT team style, Victoria and I raided our daughter's bedroom and systematically removed all her furniture (except her bed) and put it down in the basement. With huge sadness, we realized Alyssa was no longer safe with furniture in her room. We'd reached another tragic milestone in our daughter's illness.

When we first learned that Alyssa's primary diagnosis was Reactive Attachment Disorder, Victoria and I had joined several online support groups that were filled with parents who were at their own breaking points with their children. The parents in these groups also recognized that their home state wasn't going to help them, that the system wasn't going to help them, that each family was on their own to figure things out. The group members provided support where no formal support was locally available.

When you realize you are destined to live with violent, awfully behaving children, fearing for their lives, your life, the lives of your other children and pets that share the home—you come to terms with the fact that you are screwed and your outlook on life is drastically diminished.

What we experienced with our daughter confirmed for me my belief that the mental health system as it's currently designed will fail every person who needs it the most. Our story is common. You may be hearing a story like ours for the first time, but there are countless numbers of families who are dealing with the same broken system—in the same way we dealt with it, but their outcomes are not the same. Whether it's dealing with children who are sociopaths, alcoholics, drug addicted, depressed, bulimic/anorexic, or suicidal, feeling that you cannot connect with your children or help them yourself is traumatic, emotional, and overwhelming.

It's often not until a child kills or tries to kill a family member that something is done. Families shouldn't have to wait to suffer this fate before judgment-free and helpful intervention can occur. Victoria and I were living in despair. Fearing that we would have to live with this horror and hell for the next eight and a half years until Alyssa turned 18. But then what? Push Alyssa out into the world unable to care for herself? Have her end up abused, pregnant, and homeless? That's not what we wanted for our daughter, but that could easily be her future because the system is broken.

Victoria and I sat up late one night discussing our options. Sitting on opposite sides of the couch, unable to be close any longer, we saw our path ahead. Once Alyssa (who was almost 10 at the time) reached 12 turning 13, every time she was aggressive or violent, we would call the police. We would wait until Alyssa did something severe enough to warrant a legal response and pray that the authorities would think we were such a nuisance (frequent flyers on the "domestic situation" call list), that that they would put her in juvenile detention.

We knew we needed to wait until the 12/13-age milestone because until children are in middle school the police don't take these behaviors seriously. "The kids will grow out of it," their police experience tells them. "This is something parents need to handle," they believe. It didn't help that Alyssa looked like she was about six years old because she was so tiny and pretty and innocent-looking and therefore often got away with more. And the police wouldn't want to put someone so "frail" into the system and have her be eaten alive by the more substantial older children. Meanwhile, I believe that had she been incarcerated, she would have been running the detention center and guards and gotten everything she wanted in any situation.

"But what does putting Alyssa into the criminal system do?" we questioned. We answered ourselves glumly that while it gets her out of our house and keeps all of us safe, it sets Alyssa up for a future life of crime and who knows what else. And, despite all the chaos our daughter instigated in our lives, we did still love her and want her to be healthy and happy at some point.

We debated divorcing and removing me from Jackson's birth certificate, so I could take the fall for child abandonment without it impacting Jackson's well-being. We debated Alyssa and I moving to another state so that would have closer access to a residential facility should a bed become available. We were desperate for any solution to make sense.

I prayed for the Universe to take her away from us. She needed to be out of our home—out of our care. The professionals agreed she was not stable or safe living with us, but it didn't much matter because the system is so broken that, even if we wanted her to physically be removed from our house, we had no way of making that happen. The best we could do was go to the emergency room and demand her to be treated overnight on the psychiatric ward. And then what? She would come home the following day for this to happen all over again. Just how many times could our daughter take one of the limited beds available for children before something changed?

Support from relatives was gone, the neighbors were not helpful, therapy was focused on Alyssa, my wife was as overwhelmed as I was, and I had cut myself off from all but my closest friends. I needed support. As a business owner, I'd been involved in small, intimate, and confidential advisory groups of likeminded business owners with whom I'd meet regularly. I didn't feel comfortable talking to them about what I was going through at home. What would they think of me, wanting to get my daughter out of my home? But then, as my current business group was disbanding, an opportunity to join a new group surfaced.

This group was different—very different. There were eight powerful women, all of whom had different types of businesses and different religious and spiritual belief systems. As a nonreligious person and someone who didn't fully embrace the woo-woo (yet), I was anxious to be a part of this group; there was something special about them I felt drawn to. I could sense that I was going to get more from this group than just business advice.

Over time, I began sharing pieces of my personal life with them—and they with me. This group was about supporting each other as a whole, not siloed to specific business problems. The group's belief was that personal issues bleed into business and vice versa.

My business life was thriving—something I could consistently count on. My personal life, on the other hand, was a total catastrophe that I did not share with many people.

I finally found a measure of relief in sharing updates of my life with this small group of incredible women via our private Facebook Group. They became a support system in ways I didn't know I needed. I had finally found a group of people who accepted me for me and really listened to what I was sharing in relation to our home life. They never judged me. They were always there to provide endless empathy in some of the darkest times in my life. I gained strength from them. This group of remarkable women hung with me throughout all of the tough personal decisions I had yet to make. The women felt like the sisters I'd never had. I began to heal inside.

Embracing a more holistic life focus that I learned from my new sisters, I asked them, "Pray that Victoria and I can get through this together and pray that the Universe will conspire in our favor and provide us with an answer. I cannot wrap my head around another eight years of this. We are prisoners." And then we waited for the Universe to answer.

There are limited resources and support systems designed to help children with Reactive Attachment Disorder. However, one of the things recommended to us was an intensive outpatient program. We had tried the weekly and twice-weekly therapy sessions, but we needed something more intensive. There was a six-month extended-day therapy program with a great reputation. Getting on the list to be a part of this program was no easy feat. However, our situation was dire enough that we were granted a spot after a limited wait (some families wait years for these spots to become available).

I had been holding on to this glimmer of hope since May 2014, when we learned that this program existed. We knew it wouldn't be the end all, be all, because it only treats parts of the symptoms and not the core problem, but it was something. By this point, we were desperate for anything that *could* help us. We showed up at The Nook, a nonprofit organization, and walked through the doors with renewed optimism mixed with a dash of skepticism. Maybe we would be able to manage this situation and we could evolve into a functional family?

The place was dark with a lot of hallways. It looked like we were in the basement of an old church. The gloomy feeling echoed our energy at home. But we finally had hope that we would see sunlight and feel bright again.

Victoria and I went through the intake process in the program director's office while Alyssa went off to do an activity with a tall, thin, young clinician chattering away in a sing-song voice. The program director appeared worn out by too many years of working within the system. As crotchety as she was (we could understand after surviving day by day at home), we imagined that if the program director could survive, maybe, finally, we were in the right place to get a reboot for our family.

The following week, Alyssa began the first day of her six-month extended-day program. Alyssa was only three days into the program before CPS showed up at our front door.

All I could think about when I dropped Alyssa off the first morning was how she lies and manipulates every situation she is in. Her psychiatrist had told us to watch out for that when she was first diagnosed. We were praying this place, this program, would be different, that we would see progress.

The doctors/clinicians/therapists who ran the program knew what they were getting when we enrolled her. They spoke to her therapist, her psychiatrist; they read the neuro-psyche report and interviewed us for hours. No rock was left unturned; they had all the facts. We showed up with our binders of data and were as transparent as possible with *all* our information.

Alyssa, on the very first day, from the moment she walked into the building, was able to size up everyone she came in contact with. Like a high-speed computer that plays multiple chess games simultaneously, she figured out how to manipulate the situation, gain sympathy from the new specialists and staff she was to see, and she had everyone wanting to believe her version of our family stories.

If we want, for a moment, to talk about recognizing the role that privilege has in a situation like this, this is where my daughter's blond hair, blue-eyed, pale-white complexion ultimately created an adverse condition for us and her. A glance around made it clear that our daughter didn't look like the other kids in the program, most of whom were Hispanic or black boys. She was able to influence the staff with her charm; they wanted to protect her.

When you have a child exhibiting severe mental health duress, the parents are *immediately* assumed at fault, assumed to be the problem, assumed to be ignorant or neglectful. This is how the system is designed, which mostly left us feeling totally abandoned. As if to confirm our belief about the "system," using her manipulation skills, within her first three days, Alyssa had convinced the staff that we were not feeding her. And rather than ask us (or the psychiatrist, or her pediatrician, or her therapist, or the school psychologist—you get the picture), the clinical staff called Child Protective Services. So, here were so-called "trained experts in Reactive Attachment Disorder" and they just fell for the oldest trick in the RAD book—they were outmaneuvered by a nine-year-old.

To some degree, because the program failed, it would bring us a step closer to getting our daughter into the full-time residential treatment and care where she belonged. Multiple mental health professionals felt a full-time residential situation was in order but advised us that it was going to be years, if at all, before that happened. This six-month program was supposed to be a stepping-stone in that direction. And even that wasn't the end answer. But meanwhile, if we wanted a chance at a residential solution, we had to jump through hoops to have enough documented evidence to show the severity of our situation.

During our intake process, someone on the staff had proudly declared that they were "falling for her [Alyssa's] charm!" This was *not* a good sign for us. We weren't registering Alyssa for ballet class. This wasn't a popularity contest. Alyssa's manipulation skills were the exact reason we were there in the first place. We didn't want professionals to fall for her charm! We needed someone to teach our daughter to take responsibility for her actions, how to function in a family, and get her to understand that she couldn't keep hurting people.

I gave the example to the intake team that Alyssa could kill a squirrel right in front of you and … before I could finish the sentence, the program director filled in, "And I would find a way to justify her actions." YES! That's exactly right! And yet, this was from the same woman who was "falling for Alyssa's charm," the same woman who was responsible for treating our daughter, the same woman who ultimately called CPS because she believed our RAD daughter over our family and the expert testimony of the physicians and specialists we'd already seen.

When Child Protective Services showed up at our house, we were as raw, honest, and prepared as anyone could be. We always kept meticulous records of everything. So, when CPS started asking questions, we told them, "You're more than welcome to talk to Alyssa's therapist, the psychiatrist, and her schoolteacher. Here are some witnesses to the destruction she has done."

I told the CPS worker about an incident that occurred on one cold February day, a day when I had a business colleague stopping by the house. Alyssa chose that opportunity to rub her own feces all over the walls, furniture, carpet, bed, dolls' faces, etc. Before my guest arrived, I had suggested to him that it wasn't a good time, explained that my daughter was acting "worse than usual." He asserted that he had previously worked in a mental health institution and had "seen it all." Uh huh. He didn't know my daughter, but I invited him to come on by.

When he saw what Alyssa had done, he didn't judge us. He was very supportive but reiterated what we already knew: Alyssa needed to be in a residential facility where she had 24-hour supervision and a team of skilled people to care for her. I suggested that CPS contact this business associate to allow him to share what he witnessed.

Then I told the CPS agent about the time Alyssa had destroyed the floor lamps in her room, the only lighting in the space, so I hired an electrician to come in and install an overhead, indestructible, durable plastic light in her bedroom. This didn't match the décor of our elegant ceiling fan fixtures in the other bedrooms, but the electrician agreed it was a safer choice than the threat of broken glass raining from the ceiling.

The electrician had empathy for us as we explained our situation. He did everything he could to support us, which included installing a light switch for this new bedroom fixture in the hallway. With the wiring in the hallway, there would be less access to an electrical socket that could be subject to user overload, which could potentially become hazardous. We had him remove power from every socket in the room, so when Alyssa spent her days shoving paper and plastic in the socket holes, we didn't have to worry about her getting injured or setting the house on fire. I gave the CPS worker the electrician's contact information.

We handed our caseworker a sheet of paper that included the names and contact information for a long list of experts who could shed some light on our situation. We were an open book. I said, "Call my mother-in-law, she'd be more than happy to explain things to you." We made it incredibly easy for CPS to contact everyone in our lives who could be beneficial. We weren't afraid of anything a professional was going to say to them. Nothing anyone was going to say was going to contradict what we were telling them. Honesty was *the* only option.

The caseworker came to our house a couple of times and visited Alyssa at school another time. We knew this would be an open and shut case, but it didn't ease our stress and anxiety while we waited for the report to come back. This dragged out for a couple of months over the summer. We knew in our guts we had nothing to hide and that we weren't in the wrong, but even if your gut knows the truth, it doesn't mean your mind doesn't wander to every worst-case scenario imaginable.

After a long waiting period, we were alerted that we were no longer on their radar, the claims from the program could not be substantiated, and neither of our children were at risk. It was a glorious feeling to be vindicated. But that didn't actually help our situation, as we were still stuck in the same spot we were before CPS was involved. CPS came in and did their thing and we never spoke to them again. And the glimmer of hope we had of finding answers was snuffed out.

We began researching the process of relinquishing our rights. What did this mean? How do we go about doing this? It is the process of giving up our rights as parents so Alyssa could be adopted by another family. We had been through eight arduous and painful years and felt like we were spinning our wheels without making any progress. The odds were stacked against us. They are stacked against any family dealing with a Reactive Attachment Disorder diagnosis.

Virtual friends in our web-based support group recommended a book called *Relinquished: When Love Means Letting Go* by Carrie O'Toole. This book changed everything for me. We saw that the author and her family had found a solution for her son with RAD. If she did it, we could do it. We had a glimmer of hope back—maybe there was a light at the end of the tunnel.

So here I was, the queen of "getting shit done" and I couldn't "fix" Alyssa and I couldn't let her go. To relinquish our daughter meant that we were no longer in her life, no longer responsible for her, but we would also not be able to participate in any decisions on how she was to lead her life. We would not be able to communicate with her anymore unless she reached out to us. It felt very harsh and restrictive. That is not easy to accept in your heart and mind, despite how much deep down within you know it's the best solution.

Amanda relinquished her parental rights so that we could adopt her daughter, but Amanda had the right to see Alyssa every month. She had a way to know how Alyssa was doing. Amanda chose not to follow through, but the opportunity and option were there. Here, we were going to choose to be cut out of Alyssa's life forever. It was unbearable.

I wasn't ready for this. No matter how difficult life is on a day-to-day basis, even when you've been praying for an answer, giving up is a soul-crushing thing to do. We went through so much to gain custody and then to adopt Alyssa, we love Alyssa, how could we just relinquish our rights to be her parents?

I knew it was the right thing to do. I knew it was the only solution that made sense for our family. But it was eating me up inside and I was unable to commit to doing this … yet.

Age 36

A friend recommended the Adult Children of Alcoholics (ACOA) handbook, feeling certain that I would relate to much of what was in it. When I went to the website to order the book, I ended up down a few rabbit holes dropping in on a couple of people's blogs. The one thing that stood out crystal clear was that adult children of alcoholics tend to be perfectionist, all-in people. And, surprise-surprise, the example they used was running. Apparently, I am not alone. ACOAs can't just run for leisure but have to push it to extremes and run a marathon!

Reading the stories of other people like me and identifying with the characteristics of ACOAs gave me reassurance; knowing that I am not abnormal but I'm like many other people who grew up with an alcoholic parent.

Waking up every morning disappointed that I was still alive, knowing I had a battle ahead of me starting from the moment I got out of bed, I focused on running because I needed to succeed; I needed assurance that I could still overcome obstacles. Reading ACOA stories explained why I endured my marathon challenge.

Carolina and I decided to take on another Disney running event after two rain-soaked Disney half marathons. Redemption was ever-elusive, but we were giving it another shot. I needed this success. And, maybe, somewhere in the recesses of my mind, I deserved and even welcomed whatever physical pain would come. The event was a full 26.2-mile marathon. We began training in the summer for the January 2017 event.

As the weather became chillier, I had to alternate my outdoor runs with treadmill runs. The treadmill is just not the same. Passing through neighborhoods; running through town after town; and being fully engaged with nature, inhaling it through my nose and mouth and listening to the birds, dogs barking, people talking and playing, and vehicles passing feels more like I'm accomplishing something. You don't go anywhere on a treadmill. Perhaps it feels less like I am actually escaping, which was always the primary objective.

So, I pushed. And one too-cold-to-run-outside kind of day, I didn't warm up or stretch properly, ran in the cold anyway, and wrecked my knee (my IT band to be exact). From my right hip down to my ankle, if I put pressure on my foot, it hurt. Just walking hurt. But did I stop training? No. Of course not. I was running away, and no injury was going to take that away from me!

If I admitted my physical pain, if I stopped training, I would be at home; I would have to deal with the minefields of the house, so I ran on. I admitted only a small fraction of the pain I was actually feeling. I could have been ruining my knee for the rest of my life and that did not matter. Goal ahead, keep on target. I had to focus on the target to survive.

The orthopedist I finally went to see told me that the IT band had to heal on its own. I should rest it. "Sure," I promised, as I walked out into the cold and called Carolina to book our next training run date.

A month later, race day arrived. And there Carolina and I were ready to go, pain aside. We started our race around 6:45 a.m. and watched the sun come up around Disney. We passed lions and tigers stirring in the dawn mist at Animal Kingdom and spent quite a bit of time running boring miles on the closed-down highways between the parks. Despite the boring roads, every mile was filled with pure entertainment. We passed people dressed as flying pigs, the hippos from Fantasia, Tweedle Dee and Tweedle Dum, and every other Disney character ever created. We were focused on getting through the race in one piece, so trying to run in some elaborate costume was not something we could handle, but we sure did enjoy watching how creative everyone was. Our identical neon green handmade Disney running shirts were no match for the costumes we passed (or, more accurately, passed us) on the route.

At the third mile, I started to ache, by the fifth mile, entering the Magic Kingdom through the back of the castle, I was already struggling silently with pain. By the ninth mile, I told Carolina what was happening. She wouldn't go on alone without me. We kept on. I persisted. Nothing makes you feel worse than watching a man dressed in a gift box made from a family-sized refrigerator carton passing you by. And since I was already in huge pain, I just groaned aloud and started the horrible thoughts of, "What the hell did I agree to do?" I had no choice but to switch to walking at mile 17 and intermittently ran/hobbled the last 9 miles.

Weeks before we flew to Florida to run this marathon, we had altered our expectations because my knee was already an issue and we assumed there would be a problem at some point along the route.

As we neared Epcot, the last of the parks before the finish line, I was in rough shape. I was now 6 miles into hobbling and we still had 3 miles to go. The energy and the magic of running/hobbling through Epcot is that everywhere you look, there are mass amounts of people screaming, cheering, and waving you on. Strangers telling you, "You can do it! Pain is temporary! Just think of the food you can eat!" At this point for any runner, any type of hope and optimism goes a long way to get across that finish line.

Instead of finishing in our anticipated five hours, we finished in seven hours, just before the cut-off time. Our time didn't matter. We were victorious. We had trained for so long and accomplished what we had set out to do.

Within seconds of crossing the finish line, I collapsed into the medical tent and was immediately wrapped in icepacks. My triumphant finish line photo depicts an exhausted woman with no color in her face, with ice packs surrounding both knees. Definitely a photo I will treasure.

I had survived. If I could survive that and live through that pain, I was going to be able to survive my daughter and whatever challenges still were ahead of me. I would persist.

When I limped into my office the day after I returned from the race, Maya, who was now working with me in my business, gave me a commemorative necklace to mark the accomplishment. It said, "She believed she could, and she did," and it had a 26.2 charm on it. She had been the one who I told every gory detail of every training run and injury. I'm surprised she wasn't getting sympathy pains as a result of hearing about every one of mine.

My commitment to moving forward and finding help for Alyssa began by contacting an adoption agency that specialized in finding families for kids who have been adopted from the system and something goes astray, so they find themselves back in the system looking for a home again. There are only a few in the country and connecting with anyone from an agency provoked extreme anxiety. How do you call up a stranger and say that, after 10 years, you want your child to live with another family? How do you even begin a conversation like this? Clearly, this is what *they* did every day but that didn't alleviate *my* stress over making the phone call.

I finally got the courage to call one agency in particular, explained the situation we were in, provided all the background information they needed— and we were denied. We were told that Alyssa was now too old.

Too old? What? That is a thing? Yet again, optimism shattered into a million tiny pieces and pessimism became exposed again. The walls began to close in on me as I reimagined our future and the next eight years living in purgatory—our own prison. I began to have flashbacks of the things my sister did to my mother—the verbal abuse, the physical abuse, the time she totaled my mom's SUV, the black eyes, the 911 phone calls, the close relationship with the local police because they were on speed dial. I was on the edge of a panic attack trying to remain calm.

This had to work. There had to be another way. I felt defeated. I began to beat myself up—saying, "If only I had come to this decision sooner, we would have had a chance." Victoria had come around to this conclusion before I did and was ready to pursue this path, but she patiently waited for me to come to the same decision. But now that I had, it seemed that it might be too late.

It took months before I was able to pull myself together and start looking at other options. Why would I let one adoption agency close all the doors for me?

I was the hold up until this point. In the time it took for me to be ready (as ready as one can be in a situation like this), we debated simply abandoning her; calling CPS and telling them to just take her. The legal ramifications of this were unknown. I, as a business owner, was less concerned about how this made me look, as no one I did business with had any idea about the depths of chaos in my personal life. But, Victoria on the other hand, was a different story. As an educator, would she lose her license to teach and therefore her job?

Would CPS come in and demand that if we were callous (in our minds desperate was a better description) enough to abandon one child, would we abandon the other? Would they take Jackson too? We ran through all the scenarios and determined abandonment wouldn't be an option. We needed to find a way to properly relinquish our rights to Alyssa without breaking the law by abandoning her.

We were assessing. I don't like assessing. I like doing. I like getting shit done. I would work on this and find a way to make this happen. I had to. It was about survival at the most basic core level at this point. I thought about how I worked through my pain to finish the marathon and figured this was a marathon of a different kind. It was going to be longer than I planned and more painful than I could have imagined, but I would survive, my daughter would thrive in a better environment, my son would have parents who had time for him, and the pain would diminish over time and settle into a family memory.

I put my intention into the Universe and left it there. I gave myself some space to let the Universe bring solutions to me. I just had to be patient—something that has never been a strength of mine in my personal life.

I wanted my thirty-fifth year to be less anxiety-ridden. I wanted to stop using the phrases: *I hate my life. I hate our lives. I want to run away.* These are all terrible statements that I made daily as a result of our disintegrating home life, but these are not good things to put into the Universe.

Resources started appearing when I began focusing on reframing the situation. Failure to find help was no longer an option.

I am a very practical person. However, when your life feels like it is spinning out of your control, you seek answers wherever they come. While not a religious type or even spiritual at this point, I had always, deep within my being, believed that everything in life happens for a reason. Everything. This approach was employed at a younger age to make sense and meaning out of the onslaught of bad luck I was dealt in this lifetime.

So, while my Ouija board from childhood wasn't on my agenda for how to get answers, I was open to trying anything. I had my tarot cards read at one point and, retroactively reviewing my notes, the entire year was "predicted" with 100% accuracy. Even the Death Card didn't scare me when I found out that it was predicting change and that came to be in a very positive way. So, when a woman from my business group said she was practicing her ability to channel messages from the Universe for others, I offered to be a guinea pig.

Channeling, she explained, was giving her body up to spirit guides to use her to impart wisdom to someone who has a question or needs guidance. The idea, she instructed, was to ask a question of the Universe and then she would hear the answer back from my guides, God, angels, etc. and share it with me. This was completely foreign to me, but I was desperate, so I was open to anything by this point.

My question to her was, "Will I find peace in 2017?" The channeled message back was a few paragraphs long. The crux of it stated that my peace and closure was "entirely in your control." These words hit me. Hard. Once again, here I am feeling like I'm out of control and this decision is actually in my control? How was this possible?

Reframing my role in my daughter's life and removing the distress I was feeling every moment of every day for the first time in a long while, I could see with better clarity that this wasn't about me. This was about Alyssa. This was about what was in *her* best interest. The moment I could see that Alyssa leaving our care was for her best interest, I was able to make peace with actively pursuing the decision of relinquishing. My daughter's mental health needs were more than we could handle—more than most people are able to handle—and we needed to get her the help she required to give her a chance at a future. If she stayed with us, there wouldn't have been a future for any of us. This reframe was the kick I needed to step up my game to finding a solution.

That February I flew to Boulder, Colorado, for a business trip that turned into an incredible journey of self-exploration and changed my future. The workshop in Boulder was about personal branding, storytelling, and blending our business worlds and personal worlds to be in better alignment and serve a higher calling.

The process is called a "Dig" because the facilitator, Erin Weed, just keeps digging and asking question after question after question. You don't know what direction the conversation is going to go, as Erin does it intuitively. The most frightening part about this process is that she is asking these questions in front of up to 10 other people, who are listening intently to your story so they can reflect back what they hear. Every single person in the room was a complete stranger. When she was done asking the questions, you had to spin around in your chair, face the back wall, and then everyone talked about what they heard, behind your back. As horrifying as this may sound, it is done in a gentle, loving, and safe way.

My story emerged and Alyssa was part of it, naturally. Erin's intuition kept leading us down a more personal path versus the professional path I had planned on digging while there.

The manifesto I wrote (a document that expresses your desired state of beliefs) during the dig process from the feedback I heard behind my back was powerful. It brought out who I am, who I was, and who I want to be. My desire to protect others is rooted in my inability to protect myself and/or control my environment at a young age. I thought about my daughter and what she will feel when she is a woman in her thirties. Will she feel the same as I do because she is not able to control her environment now? I wanted her to be in an environment that allowed her to thrive, for I was sure that being in our home was not an ideal situation for her (or us). So, I resolved after the dig to continue to search for a solution.

For my future, I expressed through my answers a desire for freedom from myself, freedom to relax, freedom to be me, and freedom from always feeling like I needed to solve a problem. While that's the truth, of course, my first step was to solve the current problem and *then* I would set myself free.

When the dig portion was over, I got to mingle with some of the other participants, helping them to write their own manifesto. During this process, I organically made a connection with Christina. She and I went to dinner that night and she asked me more about my personal life, and I about hers.

About two months later, Christina reached out to me.

"I met a man, Eric, at this conference I just attended who mentioned that he and his wife were in the process of relinquishing and he also mentioned RAD! I never heard of this before and now suddenly both of you tell me about this within a two-month time frame! There must be a reason! Right?"

"Absolutely," I exhaled, sort of stunned.

"I think I should connect you. Eric and his wife, Corrine, have been going through this process and it seems to be coming to a good conclusion. Do you want an introduction?"

"Absolutely!" I repeated. "Yes, please!"

When I spoke to Eric soon after, he told me his daughter was six. When I heard these words, my mind went to defeat again. I thought for sure we would find ourselves at another dead end with Alyssa being too old again. When I shared this with Eric, he said, "You need to talk to Corrine. She's really the one that's active in support groups and will know who else can help you."

Corrine was very active in several online support groups specifically designed for families who are actively pursuing the process of relinquishing their rights. She invited Victoria and me to a few of them.

I joined and then hung out, reading posts, being a voyeur in these groups for a bit. One day, I got up my nerve and posted our story and asked for guidance, ideas, hope—anything!

The responses started coming in and led to us learning about an adoption agency that specifically focused on older kids. Finally! A sliver of light was peeking through the darkness pressing in around me.

Once Victoria and I connected with the adoption agency in April, we began talking to Alyssa's therapist, Lorna, about the idea. I really respected Lorna and liked her right up until she made some comments about us relinquishing our rights to Alyssa. Lorna, whose allegiance was to her patient (Alyssa), did not agree with what we had begun exploring. She made us feel that we were throwing in the towel. Everything Lorna did was supposed to be in the best interest of the child but not necessarily what was in the best interest of me, Victoria, or Jackson.

While Lorna was not originally on board with the idea of relinquishing a child, she did admit, in passing, that she had seen people "dump" their kids for less valid reasons than we had. Hearing her compare us, whether intentional or not, to parents who "dump" their kids, was yet another blow to my already emotionally fragile state.

Eventually, Lorna rallied behind us to do what we all felt was in Alyssa's best interest. The roller coaster just kept on chugging along! No one knew if we would fall off, throw up, or arrive at a beautiful destination exhilarated.

Sometimes, it only takes one thing to move you to action. With all the work I was doing on myself, I was getting ready. Then Alyssa stole my 26.2 running necklace, a gift from Maya, for having completed the Disney marathon.

That one thing triggered all sorts of flashbacks from my childhood and anger toward Amanda. All the times Amanda took my things, stole my property, destroyed my space and security with the complacency of our parents abetting her. I got fierce inside and determined that no one was going to steal my future the way Amanda had stolen my past and Alyssa was stealing my present. That necklace, which I eventually did get back, symbolized overcoming physical and emotional hurdles culminating in a huge accomplishment.

I knew I needed to be on solid emotional footing to start the relinquishing process because it was going to kick the crap out of me. At this point, I wasn't even on a C-game in my personal life, which certainly doesn't compute well with my overachiever personality. I knew I had to be on my emotional A-game.

Cindi, someone I highly respected from my women's business group, asked over lunch one day how I liked my therapist. When I said I didn't have a personal therapist, she said that, with all the heavy stuff I'm dealing with, I needed to have someone to talk to about my feelings. She promised to make an introduction to her own therapist and encouraged me to give therapy a try.

I agreed, somewhat warily, because the thought of therapy to excavate my psyche seemed absolutely terrifying. Until this point in my life, I was hell-bent against personal therapy. This distaste for the idea of therapy made no sense as I highly respected the profession. At one point during high school, I even thought I wanted to become a therapist. Thanks to my deep respect for Cindi and her personal recommendation, I anxiously gave Judy a call.

Judy, I discovered, was, indeed, a great woman. It turned out to be a relief to have someone to share all my unprocessed thoughts and not be censored or dismissed. My new therapist assured me that Pandora's box wasn't just going to start throwing more at me than I was capable of handling.

Thus, began my weekly sessions to excavate my past and prepare for a future that would, no doubt, be full of more rises and falls on the Alyssa roller coaster. I needed to start planting seeds where the earth was scorched around my childhood home and let fresh growth happen. I wanted to smell the sawdust of new beginnings as I would eventually build my new home. Judy was my personal farmer to ensure that a healthy crop, instead of weeds, would be in my future.

At one point in my journey, around the time we were starting the process of relinquishing Alyssa, I found myself sitting on the cold black leather loveseat in my living room. I was surrounded by bright yellow cheery walls upon which, to my right, a full-size black decal in the shape of an oak tree featuring large branches was affixed. On the branches we displayed photos of the kids' first days of school, a picture of Victoria and me at a friend's wedding, a few images of the kids playing outside—micro snapshots in time. It was our best effort to put forth "a normal family lives here" vibe.

I was taking a moment to myself in my otherwise chaotic house. Perched on the very edge of the loveseat, I began reciting something that resembled the Serenity Prayer, as I often did, in my head. As I allowed my body to be still for just this moment, in my peripheral vision, off to my right, something flew past me in a blur. I wasn't sure what I had seen. I thought maybe something must have moved, jostled in a gust of air.

Then it happened again and I recognized what my subconscious was perceiving. It was a big 2' × 3' blank white canvas. On the bottom left corner, against the background of the stark white canvas, I could see vibrant ferns and greenery. Not lush and overgrown, but simple, sparse, shaped like the greens at the base of a tulip. There were only a few of them sprouting up from just the one corner.

Frozen in place, time stopped for a second; I could not breathe. A heavy weight pinned my chest as a wave of panic kicked me in my gut. And when I released a breath of air, feeling like I had been hit by a speeding truck, the message I was meant to receive seemed to just be there in my head.

The green symbolized new growth, starting over. With this revelation, a cloud of calm settled over me like a flannel blanket on a cold night. I knew I was going to not just get through this complicated part of my life, but I would evolve on the other side, stronger, with more life, to bring growth to other people. I no longer felt trapped in the ether of my mind—that either I die, or she dies. With this fleeting image, the message was that we would both somehow be okay.

And then another message, in the same vein, happened a couple of days later while I was in the shower. As I was washing my hair, I was overcome by a wave of emotions. I identified grief mixed with excitement, hope, despair, and a dozen other emotions wrapped into one. It was like someone was running me over with a car. Like before, I lost the ability to breathe. When the panic passed, calm returned. I could feel in my bones that all would work out and I would somehow be fine. I didn't know how but trusted that the signs were authentic.

I interpreted these experiences as a glimpse into the future. We were getting there. It might not have felt like it at the time, but relief was coming. It was incredibly profound. I moved away from a very dark place where I felt trapped with no way out. It was the first time in years that I was starting to see the dark smoky haze lifting, signaling hope.

PART VIII

DEFEAT

Age: 36

August 2017-December 2017

Age 36

My heart was beating rapidly one late summer day in 2017. I was sitting outside anxiously waiting for my freedom. I had just gotten word about where Alyssa was going to go. It felt like it would never happen and it also felt like it would happen in 10 minutes. My heart couldn't calm down. I was going to have to wait through the next eight weeks before turning Alyssa over to her new guardians. The soundtrack for that moment played in the background of my head, "So close and yet so far away."

Getting to the day when we heard the agency say, "We have a family for Alyssa," was not smooth at all. We had many phone calls with the adoption agency itself and were panicking the entire time because it was a faith-based adoption agency. We were lesbians and we didn't know how their organization was going to perceive our situation. When one of our friends said, "Being lesbians is a gift because they are going to want to 'save' Alyssa," we exhaled. I realized that was probably true, despite being a bitter pill to swallow.

We spoke with the adoption agency throughout most of April and May, while they evaluated the case. We didn't know how long it would take or if they would even take us. It could take months, or it could take years.

Prior to a family in Kansas agreeing to take our daughter, we spent several hours on video conference calls, answering their questions, asking them questions, and basically being totally awkward and uncomfortable throughout the whole process. And all of this had to happen when Alyssa was at school or we were away from the house. She couldn't know. None of our extended family knew what was happening. It was a very lonely and confusing time. Victoria and I had only each other and that relationship was extremely strained. What parent, married couple, could ever imagine going through something like this? If I didn't have the support of my very few close colleagues, friends, and my holistic women's business group, I think I might have completely fallen apart.

Alyssa was originally scheduled to leave around Halloween, but we ran into hiccups with some interstate adoption laws. Her departure occurred in early December instead. The waiting game from October to December was absolute torture; it couldn't come fast enough. Alyssa didn't know, nor would she, until the immediate days before. We were following the consensus of advice from all the mental health professionals we were involved with, of which there were many.

I dreaded the time when I would be faced with the difficult task of explaining to Alyssa what was going to happen. I planned to tell her that she was going to go with a new family that would make her happier than we could and that we had all done our best, but she needed to be in a place where she would be safe and have a better chance at life.

When I gathered myself and when the timing was right, I asked Alyssa to sit and talk with me. I had kept her home from school the day I told her. Jackson and Victoria were at school, so we were alone. I was so nervous I had written out everything I wanted to say.

I remember saying, "Alyssa, I feel like things have been very hard for you here. We don't all get along. You seem unhappy and none of us want you to be unhappy. Mom Vee and I have been talking with Lorna and your doctors and we all think that maybe you would be better off living with a different family. We love you very much but if living here with us is making you so unhappy that you scream and cry and break things all the time, we don't want you to feel like that. We want you to be comfortable and secure." And I waited for the explosion. Nothing. Emptiness. So, I continued …

"We found a new family that is very excited to have you join them. They will come here in a few days and pick you up and take you to a new house. They have a girl around your age who will be your new sister. Isn't that great?" And I waited. I looked for signs of violence about to erupt. Nothing. But she looked pensive.

"Do you have any questions?" I asked. At first, she shook her head no.

Alyssa sat silently. She looked at me, sadness coming over her face.

Then she asked, "Where am I going?"

"You'll be moving to Kansas!" I offered infusing my voice with enthusiasm. "There are horses and cattle and lots of open space in Kansas." I told her a little more about the family and kinds of things she could expect at her new home.

"I will miss you," she said. I was pleasantly surprised. And then she continued, "I will miss Jackson and Mom Vee. I will miss Leena too." And she took a few minutes to sit in her sadness. And then it came. She started crying. Her crying gave me freedom to let loose my tears and we sat and cried for a solid 20 minutes while I rubbed her back. Her crying made me cry and my crying made her cry and on it went.

We gathered up the wad of tissues we had soaked, collected ourselves, and started to pack her bags together. This triggered another bought of equally awful crying on and off. So, we sat on Alyssa's bed and hugged and just kept crying.

After about 20 minutes, I told Alyssa I had an album the new family made and asked if she wanted to see it. She wiped her eyes and nodded yes. I got the album and we sat side by side on the bed and went through the scrapbook album they had sent. Page by page, we explored all of the things they were going to do together as a family. It was meant to help Alyssa know them a little before she met them. It included their likes and dislikes, information about their community, pictures of their home and her new school. As we turned pages, we alternately cried and talked, questioned and smiled, and cried some more. In these moments of closeness with my daughter, my heart was shredding. If we could be like this more often, I wouldn't be relinquishing her. "Why," I would beat myself up, "Why couldn't we have found a way to get to this together?"

At some point, Alyssa's face changed and I saw a spark of interest come into her eyes. It was almost like she was playing a movie in her brain and it was showing through her eyes. She sat up straight. I think she was starting to envision what living with another family would be like. She looked at me and smiled.

My damaged and bruised soul imagined that Alyssa was probably conceiving all the advantages of starting over and being able to manipulate an entirely new family and situation. But Alyssa's therapist had said on more than one occasion that Alyssa wasn't able to process emotions like a neurotypical person, so the things that are upsetting to us would make no difference in her world. Alyssa seemed to settle into the idea of going with a new family in the same way she might have if I had said we were going to buy cupcakes for a school party. And all the closeness we had shared for a few minutes seemed like a distant memory.

I picked Jackson up from school early on the day I told Alyssa. I packed the three of us into the car and we went together to see Lorna, Alyssa's therapist. It was an opportunity for Jackson, Alyssa, and I to all process together under the guidance of a trained professional. Alyssa cried. Then I cried. It was really emotional.

Later that day, we had a girls' day together. My daughter and I went to Target and I bought her clothing to wear for the plane ride and an assortment of things to do while flying—puzzles, games, and a stuffed dog. She had never been on a plane before. I went to great lengths to make sure that moving to a new place would seem to be a great process, a great transition, and that this was the best thing for her. All positive. No negatives. This *was* the best thing for her—and us.

I had been quietly packing away Alyssa's stuff for months because I knew this day was coming. I had set up the boxes and suitcase in the basement. I created an inventory list. I made a special box of all the things with sentimental value. Alyssa's new family would have a detailed list of everything that was coming with Alyssa and why it was so important to keep it with her.

Alyssa, Jackson, and I went to Chuck E. Cheese during a very nasty snowstorm to have a celebratory farewell experience. Victoria stayed at home. The two siblings had a grand old final time together. Watching them interact and play as if it would be (and may have been) the last time they would see each other broke my heart in indescribable ways. Why couldn't our life have always been like this? Why did it have to end like this?

Leaving the Chuck E. Cheese, we stopped at McDonald's and Alyssa had a Happy Meal. It was nothing that elaborate, but to Alyssa it meant the world. She seemed to be in good spirits considering all that was happening.

On the morning of her departure from our home, I was to bring Alyssa to a local hotel where Alyssa would be met and escorted on her journey with her new family. This was the first time I was meeting her new parents. We had one more small but special moment together, as I went out with Alyssa to get a donut and coffee that morning. Alyssa taking a casual ride in the car for an errand was not the norm for us, but I needed to get in every last moment I could with her, before she was swept away forever.

If we look at fight, flight, or freeze, I've always been flight. My entire life. Victoria, however, was in a freeze state. It was clear she didn't know how to process what was happening and move forward. Victoria was shut down emotionally and mentally. The send-off that Victoria provided for Alyssa didn't match what I believed should have happened. But I focused on me, on Alyssa, and on Jackson.

Due to Victoria's shut-down state, I overcompensated by trying to give Alyssa a sense that she was loved by all of us. Some of Victoria's things that Alyssa would take with her as gifts I attributed from Victoria because she loved her daughter. I believe Alyssa knew she was loved, but I wanted it to be as positive an experience as possible because these moments would likely be emblazoned in her psyche forever, if she was able to process emotions around this experience.

There were so many emotions swirling inside me as I pulled into the driveway of the same hotel we all stayed in for my wedding to Victoria. I, alone, was there to handle Alyssa's transition to the next phase of her life. We were on time—around 11 a.m. We sat in the car a moment longer than we needed to. I took a deep breath, planted a smile on my face, added some cheer to my voice as we walked together into the hotel lobby where Alyssa and I would meet her new family.

Alyssa seemed to have an aura of relief around her. I imagined she was thinking, "I can't wait to move on. Things will be better once I'm out of that house." Honestly, I was having the same thoughts. I knew my life would be better without the disruptions caused by Alyssa's RAD behaviors, but I also was torn by this huge step we were taking. And I worried for the happiness, future, and health of my daughter.

There are no guidebooks on how such an exchange should proceed. It was as awkward as you could possibly imagine. I wanted Alyssa to go, but I wanted her to want to stay; I wanted her to be happy with her new family, but I wanted her to appreciate her current family and miss us. None of this was going to happen. Alyssa doesn't feel things the way others do. She's just Alyssa. She'll always be her own unique person. I yearned for her happiness.

Alyssa had Skyped with her new family in advance. She knew what they looked like. The new family was affluent and consisted of a mom, a dad, and a daughter. Alyssa was going to have a new sister. As we crossed the lobby toward each other, Alyssa went into full-on charm mode. She could not have been any more delightful and sweet! This family was no doubt feeling so lucky, I am sure. And probably wondering what was wrong with us that we couldn't make such an easygoing child happy.

I thought it was odd that the only questions the new parents had asked us about Alyssa prior to meeting her were related to her favorite colors, foods, activities, and such, with a lot of excitement and focus on their part to get a room perfect for Alyssa, stock the house with things she'd like. It was about aesthetics. Alyssa was a pretty child, a tiny fragile thing if you just looked at her. And these folks wanted her to have a beautiful room, nice clothes, and the latest toys. Were they thinking Alyssa was a doll? Did they not understand the complexities of bringing a RAD child into their lives? Did they not know that all their lovely things would be destroyed and pulverized with glee?

They had bought Alyssa a GPS activity-oriented watch to keep her distracted while we talked and during her journey to her new home. I knew she'd have that watch completely disassembled and crushed within a few hours, but I didn't say that to them.

That's all good; physical things are nice. However, they were getting a new family member with some serious mental health issues and one would think they might be curious about how to help Alyssa fit in with their existing family structure and to help her feel supported.

The first meeting was awkward. I sat in the plush lobby area with the mother. Alyssa went up to the room with her new soon-to-be father to put her things away. The mother and I talked in short, clipped sentences. The energy I felt was that Alyssa's new mom was all about affluence and that she felt that she and her husband were saviors coming to rescue my daughter from a destitute existence. But they were not rescuing Alyssa from an impoverished situation. Nor were they rescuing a senior dog from a pound that just needed a nicer home to be happy. But it seemed to me that they were all about how material things would make everything just perfect for Alyssa.

We had prepared the new family for this transition as best we could by sharing with them 300 pages full of all the reports, school records, and medical information from Alyssa's entire life. For CPS, I had kept meticulous records and I thought the new family would benefit from all that Victoria and I had learned. You'd think they might have had a few questions about the contents of that information? After talking, I was sure they hadn't read any of it.

As I walked away, I thought, "They don't have a clue as to what they're getting themselves into!"

I left the hotel for the day but promised Alyssa I would come back and check in on her around 6 to 7 p.m. The plan was that Alyssa would spend the night with her new family at the hotel and leave with them the following day.

I spent the day crying my way through IKEA with Maya, looking at wavering lights and watery colors in every department in an attempt to distract myself from my feelings. It didn't really work. Even IKEA's trademark Swedish meatballs did nothing to make me feel better.

Alyssa spent the day with her new "mother" getting her hair and nails done, hanging out in a spa, living a life of luxury she had not been previously living. She came down to see me in a new flannel pajama outfit, spa robe, and fuzzy hotel slippers where I could see she had received a full mani-pedi and was also wearing new jewelry. Was I feeling a twinge of guilt? Did I have some jealousy that my daughter was going to have a better life without me? That she would love someone else and be a good girl for her new mom? These feelings were probably there, but I was functioning on autopilot, trying to get through this experience in one piece.

Alyssa seemed happy and content. Of course, she was. I could read her very well. Her smug look let me know that she had her new parents wrapped around her fingers and, as puppet master, was pulling their strings to get everything she wanted.

I left her there overnight. I went back the next morning to say my final goodbye to my little girl. Victoria and Jackson did not join me—they had said their goodbyes at the house the previous day. As far as Jackson was concerned, Alyssa had already flown to her new home. I was numb, going through the motions with a smile plastered on my face. "I'm making the right decision!" I had to keep telling myself. But the big thing niggling in the recesses of my mind was the huge fear that Alyssa was going to boomerang back around to us again when this new family didn't work out. I was sure they weren't going to work out. If you start Alyssa on the physical front and let her be in control, you *will never* regain control.

Could the agency that found the new family send back my daughter? Was this not really over? Was my feeling of relief only to be short-lived? This is what I thought about driving home that day.

Jackson and I scheduled a Christmas video chat with Alyssa a few weeks after she left. A stipulation was set that Alyssa and Jackson would continue to have access to one another. When she came on the screen, I knew she looked different, but I couldn't place exactly *how* she looked different. It turned out that she had gained 8 pounds in less than three weeks. Her face was bigger and her hair was shorter. She must have been eating nonstop, because gaining 8 pounds on a 60-pound body in less than three weeks is extreme. We knew she could eat until she threw up because her body had no "full" sensor to make her stop and we had shared that with the new family, but based on Alyssa's appearance, we assumed they hadn't listened.

Alyssa is a superior actress. We had no idea anything was wrong when we talked to her that day. Later, we found out that the situation at the new family's home was horrible from the moment she arrived there. We never received any specifics on what transpired but apparently there was some kind of incident between Alyssa and the new family's biological daughter. It was so upsetting that they didn't even tell the agency what it was. Shortly after our Christmas chat, this new family called the adoption agency to notify them that they had dropped Alyssa off at a local psychiatrist's office.

The psychiatrist the family had chosen for this dramatic exit didn't know anything about Reactive Attachment Disorder, which we've learned is all too common. It was an ugly scene that included a lot of back and forth between me and the adoption agency. Since the family was in another state, there was a six-month waiting period before they could formally adopt, therefore, we were still her legal guardians and thus had to be notified.

Flashback to eight years prior, I was in a similar situation when I had to get information from CPS about Alyssa and Jackson's placement after they left my sister's care. I found myself, yet again, on the phone upset and demanding information about what happened. I wasn't able to shut down and move on like Victoria seemed to have done outwardly. I still loved my daughter and needed to know she was safe.

Unfortunately, we never got the full story about what happened. I am not even sure the adoption agency ever knew what really transpired. But what we did learn is that, based on this family's behaviors, they were blacklisted from the adoption program. Everything about how they handled this seemed insensitive and must have compounded further trauma to Alyssa's already fragile state. I took such care to ensure a smooth transition and then this happened.

After the psychiatrist she was left with reached the appropriate people, Alyssa spent two nights at a hotel with female social workers while they were lining up a respite family with whom she could temporarily stay. She bounced between a few respite families but did well in each of them based on what we were told. Short-term relationships were never a problem for Alyssa.

We had no further contact with Alyssa since Christmas of 2017 until we found out in early 2019 that she had been officially adopted by a warm, loving, and giving family. Maya had, unknown to me, been watching social media for any news of what had happened to Alyssa. I don't know how she found it, but on the day the adoption was finalized (six months after they had been together) the family posted a bunch of pictures from their last six months together on Facebook. Legally, they were not allowed to post any photos privately or publicly until the adoption was finalized. I believe they unknowingly made the album public since the album included pictures of Alyssa (with a new name) in a school shirt with the name of the school and the city in which they live, which seems a bit dangerous. Victoria and I are not threats. But what if my sister was to find this information? Would she try to find her? My sister didn't know that Alyssa was no longer with us.

Simultaneously, I was smiling too, since I relished the ability to see Alyssa happy and healthy and there were photos of her enjoying new activities. She looked like she got her second start at life—which was our goal the entire time. It was heartwarming to see her thriving and soul-crushing that I was unable to provide an environment for her to thrive in.

The plan from the beginning was that we would keep open lines of communication available for Alyssa and Jackson now and in the future. The new family has our information and we have theirs, but out of respect for what they are going through, we have backed off and allowed space. When the time is right, we will be here to figure out what the new iteration of our relationships looks like.

As I was writing this book, we received a tax form advising us that Alyssa was being claimed as a dependent on someone else's taxes. Can you get any-more official than the IRS letting you know that everyone has moved on?

The next phase of our lives involved figuring out how Jackson, Victoria, and I would sweep up the pieces of the last hellish eight years and move forward with a clean slate as a family. What does family mean? What do families even look like? What do families do together? The three of us had zero concept of how to coexist in a situation where we weren't hanging on for survival. How do we go from surviving together to thriving together?

In the months leading up to Alyssa's departure, I started journaling my feelings and thoughts. It was cathartic to release my very simple dreams onto paper. I had begun imagining what my family would do when we could leave the house together. Up until the moment Alyssa would leave us, her punishment of being kept in the house was our punishment too. Soon, like a person leaving prison and imagining life on the "outside," we would be able to walk around the block as a family. We could attend a baseball or hockey game. We could even go to a friend's house and have our child play with theirs! The thoughts gave me chills of anticipation and brought smiles to my face.

Big questions with a lifetime to find the answers spread ahead of us. I was looking forward to a life that didn't involve wearing noise-cancelling headphones daily and spending weekends playing in the appliance section of hardware stores just to flee my home.

PART IX

DEATH

Ages: 36-37

June 2017-November 2018

Age 36

I learned about my mother's cancer through my uncle, her brother. He was pretty matter-of-fact about it and didn't give me a lot of information. Two close friends of mine are nurses and I was able to ask them to help me decipher the data I was provided and thus I learned the severity of my mother's diagnosis. These nurses broke the news that this was not something my mom would survive. I knew mom had less than a year to live.

I unblocked my mother's phone number and periodically checked the previously abandoned email address. If my mother wanted to reach out to me, I wanted to see the email or actually see the phone call when it came in. I was torn between leaving her to deal with her illness on her own (wouldn't she have called to tell me herself if she wanted me to be part of her life again, I wondered?) and playing the hero to go in and rescue her.

I could be my mother's savior I fantasized, but was that in my best interest? Sitting at my desk, staring out the window at the huge oak tree that protected my house, I imagined being a mother bird, swooping right in, providing final sustenance for my sick mother. I would take her on all the trips she had never gone on, go to concerts and shows she wanted to see, visit people she wanted to see before she passed. I could do all that and more for her. Make her comfortable and bring her happiness. My mother would see how successful I was. But was I? Look at my family life.

In the years since we hadn't spoken, I imagined I would be successful enough that I could anonymously pay off my mother's mortgage and not tell a single person I had done it. Despite not being there to take physical care of her, I still felt a strong desire to protect her.

My gut reaction was that I felt I *had* to step in and do this. But when I slowed down to think and feel what do I really *want*, these two things did not match. I quickly realized what a rough and vulnerable spot I was in. I just couldn't take on any extra hate or anger that my mother might have left to dump on me.

I think this need to protect her started young. When I was around 14, I became my mother's caregiver. She had an accident at the hospital where she worked that shattered many bones in her foot. After countless surgeries, the bones never healed right, leaving her not nearly as mobile as she once was. I did the household grocery shopping while she waited in the car outside for me. When I learned to drive, I eventually did more of her errands and took her to doctor's appointments. She had a rough life and she needed someone to care for her.

But it was this line of thinking that was so dangerous to the future of my well-being. I could see that I needed to remain disassociated for my own survival. I had to be strong for the kids. I had to be strong for my cool and distant spouse. I had work responsibilities. Just when could I don that cape and do my swooping? It wasn't going to work. It was a hard decision to come to—to not be there for my mother as she was actively dying, but it was the right thing to do for me in that moment. Sometimes we have to be selfish out of sheer self-preservation.

I had a window of time between August and December before Alyssa left to make up my mind about letting the kids see their dying grandmother. With the knowledge of how aggressive my mom's form of cancer was and how little time she likely had left, who would it benefit and who would it hurt if the kids saw their Grammy?

At this point, the kids hadn't seen their Grammy in four years (since the birthday showdown). Victoria and I never poisoned the minds of the kids in regard to their grandmother. It wasn't fair for me to spew my disdain and drama with my mother onto them. Yes, we removed the kids from her life, but I believe we did so in a minimally dramatic way. They still loved their Grammy and believed I did too.

Something was telling me not to do it. Honestly, I was afraid Amanda would try to kidnap the kids. My mother and sister always had a volatile relationship—always. It was a constant living together, getting kicked out, moving back in, then getting kicked out—vicious cycle on an endless loop. At this point, Amanda was living with my mother, taking care of her actually. I will be forever grateful that for all her faults and flaws, my sister admirably stepped up to care for my mother in her last nine months.

Victoria wanted nothing to do with all of this and deferred to what I wanted to do. She didn't think it was in the kids' best interest for them to see their grandmother, but still left the decision up to me.

I didn't want the last memories my kids had of Grammy to be of a sick and dying woman. I would rather them think of Grammy as they last saw her. My mom was a loose cannon. We ran the risk of her telling them she was dying or saying something else inappropriate. It was self-preservation, yes, but I was also protecting my kids, doing what I felt was best. They would not see their grandmother I decided. But then that left me. What was I going to do about seeing my mother?

One day in December, about six months after the original cancer diagnosis, my cousin Kate called me. She and I don't communicate outside of family events.

Kate told me that my mother had taken a turn for the worse and didn't have much time left. She pleaded with me daughter-to-daughter so I wouldn't have any regrets about not reconnecting before my mother died.

After I asked about my sister being in attendance, Kate said I should focus on finding peace and not worry about my sister.

This emotionally intense conversation was enough incentive to get my butt into the car. I went alone, a couple of days after Christmas.

I visited my mother in a short-term residence/nursing home about two hours from my home. I felt I had to go. Despite my therapist telling me I didn't have to do it unless I wanted to do it, I still went.

Alyssa had left our home only a few weeks before and I was not in the best emotional condition when I arrived at my mother's bedside. I had pulled together tokens of affection and toys as gifts and told my mom, "Oh the kids miss you so much." I had gathered these things from my family without the kids or Victoria knowing. This whole episode was very challenging emotionally for me to summon the strength to keep a brave face and lie to my mother.

But, despite blocking her out of my life, I found I still wanted my mother to feel loved. I wanted her to die knowing that her grandchildren loved and missed her. She needed to know that I loved her, even though I didn't agree with her behaviors for much of my life. And maybe I needed to know that she still loved me.

Was I projecting what I hoped my kids would feel about me when I was older onto how I should treat my mother? Was there some kind of mother-to-mother bonding thing happening? I don't know. I was doing what I had to do, wherever that instinct was coming from.

When I arrived at the nursing home, I saw my mom's car with a "Fuck Cancer" sticker in the back window, so I knew Amanda must be driving the car. Amanda, always inappropriate, was parked in the handicap spot and I know it was not because she had just been bringing my mom in or out of the facility. I also knew that this meant she was there visiting and I wasn't going to be able to see my mom alone.

I walked down the mock-cheery holiday decorated hallway with an indescribable level of anxiety. Step by step, as I counted down the room numbers toward my mother's room, I worried that my robust mother was wasting away as cancer ravaged her body. I didn't know what to expect.

Through the open door, I could see Amanda sitting in a chair near the bed. It had been seven years since I'd last seen her. She hadn't changed—not that I expected her to. She looked toward me as I walked in the room. I watched my sister's face fast-forward through a rainbow of thoughts and finally settle on a look of disgust. I felt the same.

As I turned my head, I saw a small, frail woman sitting in a chair beside the bed. My mother's eyes settled on mine, she smiled. Someone yelled, "Blast from the past." I hadn't given them advance warning—I just showed up. I walked in.

Amanda nervously launched into a ramble about how she killed my mom's plant and we made more small talk despite neither of us wanting to. She made dumb comments and I retorted; the usual banter of two people who couldn't stand to be in the same room their entire lives.

I had mentally prepared an elaborate story for my mother; a lie about both kids and how they had made handmade gifts for her. I lied like it was my job, even though lying is something I am notoriously bad at. I handed my mother a stuffed Red Sox Pillow Pet Jackson had gifted me for my birthday followed by a jewelry box Alyssa had made for me at some point. I told my mom these were from her grandchildren and they said they hoped she feels better.

I showed my sister and mother a picture collage I had made but said the kids and I had worked on it together. I feigned interest in what my sister thought about seeing pictures of the kids, but didn't say much. Then she, thankfully, left. Our whole time together was an interminable 20 minutes.

As my mother and I tried to cover the awkwardness of being together for the first time in five years with chitchat, I made note of the multitude of drains and ports coming from different places and hoses peeking out of her clothing. Despite having lost most of her hair, my mother didn't look as bad as I was expecting. I stayed with my mom for another three hours primarily catching up like two neighbors talking over a fence. My mother shared general family news and issues. Who else has cancer, the status of her friends' mental health condition, etc … Nothing significant, but I think it made her feel better to update me on all the family and friend gossip.

At one point, an attempt was made to find answers as my mother asked why I didn't reach out to her in the years we had been estranged. Why didn't I want to share my life and what had been going on? I answered calmly, with no rancor, "Because I don't have room in my life for your judgment. Or anyone's for that matter." Then we went back to small talk. She didn't try to fight with me.

My mother dropped the bomb that Amanda was pregnant again. Baby number four. She said that Amanda didn't want me to know she was pregnant. I said I've got sources and already knew—which was true. Social media is a revealing place—not much is kept secret.

My mother filled me in on future plans. She would leave the nursing home in mid-January and go back to her own home where Amanda would continue to take care of her. Amanda, my mother said, quit her job to become our mother's caregiver. For everything horrible I have noted about Amanda in the entirety of what I've relayed to you—I will give her credit for dropping everything to take care of my mother when she was needed. She did something I was unable to do.

I didn't tell my mother much about me or the kids but shared an elaborate story I'd concocted about why I came alone. I assured my mother that the rest of my family all sent their love.

Before leaving, I helped my mother put on her pants because she needed to change for physical therapy and she couldn't manage a change of clothes herself. This was something I had done many times in the past. As I moved to leave, my mother reached out, put her hand on my arm, and quietly asked, "Can we call a truce?"

My brain was calculating ... her updated prognosis in November was about six months, so by May she could be gone. At that moment, looking into her watery eyes, I felt that if I saw her again, that'd be okay. I felt at peace for whatever would come next. If my mother called, I might answer. If she needed something, I might help. But I could now sleep knowing I showed up. Even if just for three hours.

I walked to my car after seeing my mom, feeling lighter having gone. It was pretty uneventful. It was like old times. Honestly, it was the best-case scenario because I did not back down and was firm in everything I'd previously said, but I was also civil, nonconfrontational, and compassionate.

My mother had threatened to haunt me my entire life upon her death if she wasn't buried with the cremains of Bub (her white and orange beloved cat). Now, she wanted this Red Sox pillow from Jackson buried with her too. I would have moved mountains to ensure Bub was with her in the afterlife. I worked to ensure that both the Red Sox stuffed pillow and her beloved Bub would be placed in her casket before it closed for the last time.

Toward the end of my mom's short nine-month battle with cancer, Victoria decided we should separate. I knew she wasn't in a good place; I could sense it. I kept asking her what was wrong and she'd respond, "Nothing." One day in the end of February, I pleaded with her to tell me what was wrong. I said, "I don't care if you need to write it down because you can't verbalize it, but please let me in." A few days later, she shared a Google Doc with me that expressed all of her feelings—the end conclusion was that she needed time and space away from our marriage.

It felt like it came out of the blue, but it made perfect sense. Our relationship had been focused on overseeing Alyssa, keeping Jackson safe from Alyssa, managing our home, and keeping ourselves as sane as possible, given all our circumstances. Then we focused on Alyssa leaving and coaching Jackson through the transition. Our focus was always on others and never the two of us. We never even had a honeymoon.

I cried for a day and then resolved to move on. I truly knew (and know) that it was the right decision for both of us. We continued to live together for a number of months following the declaration, as we began to uncouple the life we had built together.

The timing of this declaration felt terrible. I started wondering, "Couldn't you have told me this six months ago, Victoria, when I had time to repair my relationship with my mother?" I had chosen Victoria over my mother in many instances (which doesn't change how my mom treated me or her), but I began thinking, "I chose you over her and now you leave me and my mother is months from dying. And I have had no time to fix that relationship because I've been investing all my emotional and physical energy in us, our family, and in Alyssa—just to survive."

A good portion of my identity was wrapped around being in a marriage. Taking off my wedding ring left me feeling naked. The empty finger was foreign. I hadn't left the house without the ring in seven years. There were times I'd start to drive down the street and realize it wasn't on because I tended to fidget with it around the steering wheel. I would take the extra time to go back and get it.

It was about three months from the time Alyssa left to the time my wife declared separation. The only way I can describe it is that we all know the earth orbits around the sun. Alyssa was the sun, and we were the earth. The sun went out and gravity no longer held us together. We had drifted so far apart during our eight-year battle with Alyssa that it wasn't until she was no longer in our lives that the spotlight shone on how damaged our marriage was as a result.

The evening before April Fool's Day, my sister called me in a panic, telling me that this was the end—that I needed to get there right away. The challenge was that I was in Atlanta at a book launch event for one of the authors I worked with and was scheduled on the first flight out in the morning. Amanda believed that if I was able to get there the following day I would make it in time.

On Easter Sunday, April 1, I woke up, packed my bags, and headed to the Atlanta Airport. Again, donning my Unabomber-chic style of hoodie, hat, and jeans, I wept behind my dark glasses the entire flight, chugging down bottles of water. I arrived in my layover city of Baltimore midmorning. I recall standing in front of the departures sign and questioning if I should try to switch my flight to head directly to Providence instead of Hartford, knowing that as soon as I landed in Hartford, I would need to drive two-hours east. My logical brain advised me to just stick with my existing flight because I'd be able to stop at home, get a change of clothes, and then have my own car, since I didn't know what the coming days would bring.

I picked up my car in the long-term parking lot at the airport and drove straight to my house. It was like a pit crew stop. I went to the bathroom, gave Jackson a quick hello and a hug, and, when I came out Victoria handed me a bag she had packed for me and I was back in the car. I was in and out within 10 minutes.

Driving as fast as I safely could, I was burning rubber along the Massachusetts Turnpike trying to get to my mother in time. "Amanda is always so melodramatic," I thought, "I will get there on time. Calm down!" I needed to stop the tears because it was like trying to drive through a rainstorm with no wipers.

I was shaking, barely functional and my mind started wandering and questioning. Had I made the right choice in only visiting my mother once after she got sick? Was I a good daughter? Did my mother know I loved her? Did I honor my family by choosing my marriage over my mother? The doubts and recriminations started flying around in my head like I was being attacked by bees—stinging me with jolts of regret.

I spoke to Amanda for a few minutes. We cried together and then I said I had to stop crying so I needed to get off the phone. She sounded relieved that I was on the way.

I called Victoria and dry heaved and intermittently sobbed the entire rest of my drive, somewhere in my mind reassured that if I drove off the road, I was on the phone with her and she could dial for help. Sadly, this is a common thought I have.

When the GPS said I was 36 minutes from my mother's hospice bed, my sister called to tell me my mother had just passed. I didn't make it. Amanda wasn't there either. She had gone to pick up stuff from the house. I'm still not sure what to make of this. I missed her by just 36 minutes—I happened to be 36 years old. The numerical significance of this struck me.

I got to the hospice center and waited for my sister in the lobby. We hysterically cried, hugging in the lobby before getting ourselves together to go upstairs. We hadn't hugged like that in our entire lives. And now that my mother is gone, I don't know if we'll ever be together like that again.

Growing up, I disliked the Easter holiday, primarily because of the religious component. When my dad died about a month before Easter in 1997, I really hated the holiday. My mother died on Easter Day, which, in 2018, happened to also be April Fool's Day. It is not lost on me that my mother chose to leave this earth on April Fool's Day, without either of her children by her side. She was best known for her loud cackle of a laugh that could embarrass her children. You could hear her in the bleacher seats from the other side of a softball field and my teammates all knew that laugh was attached to my mother. I feel like my mother laughed one more time from beyond. The ultimate April Fool's prank.

I expected the worst, preparing for my mother's funeral arrangements. Amanda and I have never been able to do anything without drama in our lives. But we came together in a most impressive manner. A cousin of ours was named the executor of my mother's will, so we were fortunate to have a mediator present should we need one. We civilly chose the funeral music, the prayer cards, the hymns that would be sung, the flowers—everything was decided without contention.

I believe the best thing we did together for my mother was send her off with the kind of bang we knew she would appreciate. Growing up, my mom's favorite holiday was Halloween. What our family did for Halloween was half of what other families did for Christmas. As a nurse, my mother had a bendable Halloween skeleton decoration that she dressed up for all holidays. His name was Skelly. Her friends would sew different seasonal outfits for Skelly. The one costume I remember vividly was the Santa ensemble. We aren't 100% sure where the original Skelly went, as we couldn't find it in my mother's possessions, so I looked to Amazon Prime to get a replacement Skelly for the wake.

I learned that one of my mom's dying wishes was to make it to baseball's Opening Day, which was three days before she passed. I went to Target and purchased a Red Sox jersey meant to fit a 12-month old and dressed Skelly II in Red Sox attire. Additionally, I made him his own baseball card claiming him the mascot of her previous nursing unit. I knew many nurse friends would be in attendance and it felt the best way to honor my mother.

The logistical challenge was to figure out where to hang a skeleton in a funeral home. I made Victoria hold him while I coordinated with the funeral home director. We were able to get a choir robe and the stand that holds the hymnbook and we hung Skelly II above the guest book. Those who knew the inside joke really appreciated it. Those who didn't know the backstory of Skelly still knew of my mom's warped sense of humor, so they had a chuckle too.

At the wake, before I left her for the last time, I said aloud to her open casket. "I'm sorry and you were right." Because I do think my mother was right about a lot of things she picked up on in my marriage and maybe with my daughter. She wasn't right about the birthday cake, but we could have worked out the other stuff if we had time. I felt better forgiving my mother, rather than feeling like our whole relationship was all for naught. There was good in her too and owning that made me feel better.

The Book of Forgiving by Desmond Tutu and his daughter talks about the incredible healing power of being able to forgive even the absolute worst things about others in our lives. It's not for the person you are forgiving but for yourself. To heal. And I'm finally understanding a little bit of how that has worked for me—and still knowing this will be a lifelong journey of healing.

About a week after my mother's funeral service, I was in New York City for a speaking engagement—the first professional thing I attempted to do after her death and as the dust began to settle. I was staying in the same hotel I had stayed in multiple times before. There was no reason this environment in particular would cause me any sleeping duress. However, the night before my speech, I found myself completely and utterly unable to fall asleep. In the morning I passed it off as a fluke incident and went about my day.

Rather than heading home from NYC, I was flying directly to Milwaukee for a client engagement. When I arrived in Milwaukee, I was relieved to be in a clean and spacious hotel room, compared to the tiny NYC shoe box I slept in a day before. I thought for certain, I would catch up on the lack of sleep from the previous night. However, I was wrong.

This sleep deprivation ordeal began on April 12. My body had completely shut down and was unable to sleep—at all. I started off adding melatonin (all natural, right?) then trying my go-to over-the-counter drug (Nyquil PM) and, when that didn't work, I went through all the other PMs (Advil, Tylenol) and then Benadryl. Still no luck.

Sometime in mid-May, not having slept for a month, I was miserable and desperate for sleep. Despite craving my former nine hours, I was only able to sleep for about 90 minutes on *some* nights. I contacted an APRN at the advice of my therapist to at least explore my options with Big Pharma. I've never been a fan of Big Pharma. My APRN was conservative in her prescriptions, which is exactly what I was looking for.

Between mid-May and August, I tried a bevy of prescription sleep medications and I was still sleepless. The APRN suggested I add different supplements into my daily routine. In desperation, I tried combinations without concern for side effects, but nothing made a dent. I was barely functional.

I proactively went to all possible doctors and had annual check-ups to rule out any underlying cause that could be contributing to my body's inability to sleep. Everything came back fine. All things considered, my body's physical health was in great shape.

In June, a few friends were telling me how meditating can really help with sleep troubles. After doing some research, I opted to learn Transcendental Meditation (TM). While it didn't help me sleep directly, I could feel the calming effect it was having on my body by meditating once in the morning and once in the afternoon daily. A practice I maintain today. TM helps me with creativity and stress reduction.

One of the more holistic modalities I tried at the urging of a friend was Reiki, a technique that practitioners use to move universal energy to promote emotional and physical healing. I was warned in advance about all of the things I would feel in my body. I felt nothing.

I was not getting proper sleep and was moving into a completely non-functional state in all areas of my life.

Eventually, in the fall, I found myself at a naturopath's office, at a friend's recommendation. She ran cortisol tests to see where the deregulation in my sleep was occurring. And the results came back shocking. She said it was no surprise I wasn't able to sleep because my cortisol levels were completely off the charts. My body was shutting down because of the overwhelming amount of stress within it. Apparently—losing your child, your mother, and having your marriage fall apart in the span of four months will do that to you— who knew?

The naturopath gave me a variety of different supplements to take to work on rebuilding my cortisol levels back to a normal level. By October 21,

I was sleeping again. I had gone 192 days without proper sleep. You learn a lot about what is important to focus on versus what isn't when you only have a small window of time during any given day to be functional. This experience fundamentally changed me.

Hard reality set in when I realized that I was an orphan at 36 years old. I've jokingly said to friends over the years that, despite having two families (adopted and birth), I've always felt like an orphan. But it's different when it actually is the truth.

With Alyssa gone, I couldn't simply show up to a family gathering without there being an elephant in the room. For one, we've taught Jackson not to lie, so to try to get him to keep a secret about his sister not living with us anymore is an unfair burden to put on a child. Second, no one in my family knew we relinquished our daughter—until now, as they are perhaps reading this book. Third, my wife and I were no longer a couple and she had no reason to attend my family gatherings. I had to figure out how to fend for myself because no one was looking out for me—which oddly felt like the story of my life.

I was mostly alone by choice. I had all my friends, my clients, my team … there were people around me. I still shared the house with my soon-to-be ex-wife. My son and my cat still provided love and amusement. But suddenly I felt abandoned and truly alone for the first time.

I went from a married family of four to a soon-to-be divorcee parent of one. I resolved to focus on the logistics—something I can control and am good at. Who needed to know this change-of-status information?

I find it unsettling and hard to swallow when someone asks me about having children and I stumble over, "Yes, I have two, no I mean one child."

Having to think before speaking; having my elevator-pitch ready with the story I am comfortable sharing with the world.

I had to update my bios for business and personal social media. I focused on being vague. Instead of saying, "Lives in Connecticut with her wife and their two children." It was now "Lives with her family in Connecticut." Those I knew before this all happened may ask about the "kids" and I have to update them. I tell people who meet me for the first time that I have one child. When those worlds collide, things can get awkward. I'm back in the world of "covering" a major part of who I am. I am partly back in the closet, but for a whole new reason.

This happens far too often. And, to make matters more difficult, I've written five nonfiction books, all of which mention my family of four, so it's out there. My worlds collide regularly and for that and many other reasons, I felt I *needed* to write this book.

Part of me wants to share the whole story and unburden myself. The more I share, the less pain it causes in me. But do people want or need to hear this? Not everyone. But some people will want to know what it was like because they will see themselves. I want to encourage people to not give up. Your current situation may not end the way you want or think it should, but you can reboot and take a different journey, respond in a different way; when you're ready.

In fall 2019, while writing this book, I was sponsoring an event on behalf of my business where three different people from three different times in my life who I hadn't seen in years all simultaneously happened to be in the same room with me. One of the women, a life coach, approached me and inquired cautiously, "Can I ask you how everything turned out?" I just blurted out, "Well, Alyssa is in a new home with a new family and I'm divorced." She reacted, "WHAT?" Explaining what had transpired was some kind of surreal closure where I recognized how far I had come and that I had moved on. All the loose threads of my life were pulling together to finally form a beautiful fabric.

PART X

DETERMINATION

Ages: The Rest of My Life

Present Day

Present Day

From the time of the fire that destroyed my childhood home until these disparate people collectively helped me recognize how much I have grown and evolved, I didn't see the future. Now, I see that I have the ability to begin again. To be a catalyst for change and growth in the world. To help my fellow humans. To heal the earth. Like the vision I had about the canvas with greenery, from the ashes of the scorched wood, new green will grow and be cultivated into something beautiful, organic, and evolving. What an inspiring and motivating focus. I had to hit the bottom to regain clarity and understand my soul's purpose on this earth. After all, nothing happens without a reason. I am a more whole person now with a lot more clarity.

Even just being clear about where you want to go in your mind without sharing it with others will help you get there with less struggle. Whatever adversity you face or people you need to interact with who are not acting in your best interest ... stop, assess the situation, look deep inside yourself to envision the future as you'd like it to be, and the plan will come. The Universe will align (if you are acting for the good of the earth and humans) and you will eventually arrive at your desired destination.

Be forewarned, the journey may not look like you intended. Some things may make no sense. Some steps may not be easy. You may feel you're getting off track or being detoured. But rest assured, you are learning what you need to learn, meeting the people you need to meet, having the experiences you need to have—to achieve your life's purpose. You've heard it before and it may be a cliché, but I truly believe nothing happens by accident.

To be honest, NO ...

- I did not enjoy having my house burned down and losing my beloved cat and belongings.
- I did not want to figure out my sexuality while entangled in sexual assault situations.

- I did not put having to adopt my sister's children and then having to relinquish one of them on my bucket list.
- I did not intend to get divorced or to become a single mother.
- I did not dream about finding family, creating families, only to feel estranged from them all.

For LGBTQ+ people, self-identifying, then coming out and sharing this news with the world can be overwhelming. It can be bumpy, smooth, or anything in between. Acknowledging that I am a lesbian to my family and the world was the *least* of the issues I have faced in my life. And I absolutely recognize that I am saying this from a place of privilege. As a petite, white, ginger who can pass for straight, I am able to boldly declare that my sexual orientation has had less to do with my struggles than so many other things in my life.

Now that I've told you my story—I don't want you to feel bad. I don't want you to tell me how sorry you are. I don't want you to say you wish you could change my past. I didn't share this with you as a "woe is me" sob story.

I shared this with you because I need to be *seen* for all that makes me, me. And I know that there might be something you are going through where you may also feel the need to be seen. And my strong desire is for you to step into the light and help others also feel seen.

I've created a private page on my website for you, which you can visit by going to http://www.jenntgrace.com/hof. You'll find reading materials, printable book club questions, mental health resources, and even my TEDx-style talk I did about my experiences 18 months before I thought I would publish this book.

Our struggles may be different, but they can be the things that unite us. Please open your heart and allow it.

A Letter to the Reader

Dear Reader,

Thank you for making space in your life for me to share mine with you.

What I share in this book is written for you, the person struggling in isolation with your invisible (or secret) story that weighs on your mind, in your heart, and in your soul. I implore you to use this book as a way to connect with someone who may not understand your struggle.

It has been written for you, but I also urge you to pass it along to that person in your life who may be judging you. The old adage is the person furthest away is the one who is listened to the most. Let me be that furthest person for you and your struggle.

We are often surrounded by people who just don't "get it." My hope is this book helps them "get it" for you, so you can exist without the immense judgment from those around you.

The entire struggle we went through with Alyssa was primarily private. I didn't post my woes to social media about everything going on. I just couldn't. Other people couldn't understand. Our life was the stuff of made-for-TV movies. On the surface, my life and business looked perfect—a carefully curated image. We had several groupings of friends who were along for the ride with us, who knew the darker truth, the reality.

When I look back, I needed to talk, share, and vent, but I recognize that I pushed people away because I didn't know how to ask for help without feeling like I would look weak. It was hard to open up because I felt judged. I never knew who was a safe person to share my story with. Imagine a world where people didn't try to fix us, but just accepted us.

You never know what challenges someone faces in their head, in their home, at their office, within their family. I wish that before people cast judgment based on what they think they know about someone standing in front of them, that they take a moment to look for who that person is authentically. Try to see the not-so-obvious layers of identity; understand that people struggle with private issues (mental, physical, emotional, financial, familial, etc.) without sharing that in the world. Being kind to others and attempting to understand unseen struggles is part of my new mission.

For you, I hope there's no one in your life (family or friend) who is bringing you down with their interpretation of how you should live, be as a family, or be seen in this world. I hope you find the courage to speak your truth and to take care of yourself along the journey. Family and friendship are not always what we are born into, but rather what we create.

I believe my desire to protect others, to share other people's lessons learned to provide clarity, vision, and leadership for fellow humans is rooted in my inability to protect myself and/or control my environment at a young age.

This was a catalyst to my founding Publish Your Purpose Press. The experiences you've had in your life give you the tools to help and support others going through their challenges. Step up. Be there. Use your wisdom and past to help others. I passionately believe the more raw and real we can be—the deeper the connections we can experience. This drives my fierce commitment to bring voice to the invisible stories that free people from their isolation.

A friend said to me, "You are publishing books as a way of healing yourself through others."

Now, I've healed myself more by being raw and real and sharing my story in all of its messy glory. I ask you this: What are you doing to heal yourself while also making space and being there for others in the process?

Please connect with me. I am here to listen.

Yours truly,

Jenn T Grace

The Birth of Publish Your Purpose

In the fall of 2015, while building a jigsaw puzzle over the Thanksgiving holiday, I had an "aha" moment. I've always loved puzzles, dating back to when I was younger and trying to block out the sounds of my mother and sister screaming. They are the thing that has kept my hands and mind occupied in the desperate moments where I wanted to run away from my life. When I am building a puzzle, I'm able to block out everything around me and laser-focus on the task at hand. I'm sure this was somehow tied to control—I was doing something I was able to control (a puzzle) while my world fell to pieces around me. I later learned, thanks to my wonderful therapist, that I was likely disassociating during these times—and at many other times throughout my life.

While thinking about how much I hated my life and how alone I felt, I had an epiphany. There are so many people who don't have the wherewithal or the means to tell their story—how different would the world be if we were able to share the sordid details of how traumatic and complicated our lives are? This gave more meaning to the questions I asked myself daily: Why am I going through all of this? What lesson do I need to learn in this lifetime? How do I need to use this experience to help others? I was down a rabbit hole of self-reflection.

Working on the puzzle—piece by piece—brought new revelations about challenges of everyday people suffering in silence. I wanted to help people share and provide a way for them to help and support each other. I resolved to figure out how to do that.

In my professional life as a business coach and consultant, I worked with many authors in both formal and informal capacities over the years. The combination of realizing I had worked with a lot of authors guiding them on how to tell their story and aiding them in pushing further in sharing their truth—and realizing that if *I* felt powerless and voiceless to share my truth around my daughter's Reactive Attachment Disorder (RAD) diagnosis (which explains the screaming in the background that brought me to the puzzle world in the first place), then how did my newly acquired online support group of RAD caregivers feel? I imagined they felt trapped, stuck, like there was no way out, that there was no light at the end of the tunnel—just like me.

The RAD family stories we encountered were bleak and packed with raw emotions of (mostly) women just trying to survive. Thriving wasn't even an option for anyone—it was survival mode, 24/7, for hundreds of other families just like ours. I thought about all the other families facing challenges around illness (mental and physical), finances, issues of faith, family dysfunction, trauma … Where do they go for support? How do they learn they are not alone?

The concrete manifestation of figuring out my inner puzzle was that I wanted to start sharing and publishing other people's stories. Having people realize they are not alone, being inspired to create, build, and heal … it would all be good for the Universe and good for me to work in a positive direction. I had the access, means, and ability to pull this off—I felt called to do it.

I glanced up from the puzzle, across the room, to a shelf where I had filled a 4-inch three-ring binder with all my notes, reports, assessments, etc. that tracked the progress of my daughter's education needs and mental health care. It was unwieldy to track health stats and medication changes. The first book project that came from my epiphany was a workbook/journal Victoria and I co-created called *Therapy Notes for Families: Staying organized with your child's needs.*

The book was designed to help parents in situations similar to ours stay more organized regarding their children's mental health needs. Balancing dozens of different doctor, therapy, or psychiatry appointments in any given month becomes overwhelming, so we created this book for ourselves and turned it into a resource from which others could benefit.

This "aha" moment turned into a full-fledged book publishing company centered around purpose and helping people tell their stories. The book you are reading is part of my personal mission to give voice to the voiceless—and share my truth.

I *need* to help people tell the stories that other publishers may not want to or may not be as passionately committed to telling. We need to hear voices from all communities of people, so we can learn, share, and grow as human beings and leave the world a better place than we found it. We need to read stories that help free us from the things that isolate us.

My goal is to give marginalized voices power and a stage to share their stories, speak their truth, and impact their communities, while elevating voices from diverse communities who have faced any number of adversities in their life. If you look at the Publish Your Purpose Press (the publishing company I founded in 2016) catalog of books, you will see common themes of people using their personal—and sometimes tragic—experiences to pave the way and make the path clearer for someone behind them. This is my life's purpose and why I exist.

I've always believed that *Everyone Has a Story*, but the real courage is everyday people standing up and telling theirs. I invite you to share your story with me because the best way to heal our traumas and ourselves is by being heard and feeling seen. Please, email me at jgrace@publishyourpurposepress. com to share your story with me. I am here to listen.

Acknowledgments

There are so many people who are to be thanked for helping me along on this journey.

To Fern Pessin for her ability to help me bring my story to life. I would not have been able to do it alone. I am forever grateful for your patience and commitment. This has been one heck of a ride together and it's only just begun!

To my ride-or-die, who was by my side in the trenches through the majority of these ordeals and truly kept me sane when I thought I was anything but.

To my longest friendship, my pseudo-sister, and running partner, you kept me going when times were bleak. All of our running jaunts were therapy for me on so many levels.

To my therapist, I don't know what I would have done without having a safe space and safe outlet to get through all of these times.

To the extraordinary women who were part of my holistic women's business group. Without your unwavering support and judgment-free space, I am not sure I would have survived. I am forever grateful to each of you.

To my ex-wife, despite how things turned out for us, you are the only person I would have chosen to be on this mental health roller coaster with. If only we had had a chance.

To my son, for reminding me to act like a kid once in a while and that our bodies and minds are nimble and can overcome the traumas of our past.

To my sister, for all of the bad that has been spoken within these pages, I am grateful that you allowed me to raise the children you gave birth to and give them a better life. It was a selfless act regardless of how the events unfolded.

To the Publish Your Purpose Press team, especially my editors, without your steadfast brilliance in helping me craft this story, this would not be the piece of work that it is. I am forever indebted to your generosity in your approach and commitment to getting *House on Fire* in the hands of the readers who need to hear this story the most.

To all of my early readers, your feedback was instrumental in ensuring my story came across in the most cohesive and impactful way.

About Jenn

Jenn T. Grace is a nationally recognized business strategist, speaker, and author. Guided by the mantra, "Change happens in business," Jenn believes social change happens first in the workplace before spilling over into mainstream society. She has been featured in *Forbes*, *The Huffington Post*, *The Wall Street Journal*, and CNBC.

Passionate about helping people share their stories of adversity, Jenn is the Founder of Publish Your Purpose Press, a publishing company that includes the PYP Academy, with programs that teach aspiring authors how to publish their books. In addition to publishing 50+ books that share the stories of others, Jenn has written six.

You can follow Jenn on social media at—

Twitter: www.Twitter.com/JennTGrace
Facebook: www.Facebook.com/JennTGrace
Instagram: www.Instagram.com/JennTGrace
LinkedIn: www.LinkedIn.com/in/JennTGrace

Hire Jenn to Speak

Make an impact at your next event with Jenn T. Grace as your keynote speaker.

She has spoken on a variety of topics ranging from LGBTQ+ inclusion in business and the workplace to leveraging the power of your personal brand by being uniquely you to how we can lead with empathy.

Jenn is a gifted storyteller and her speaking style has been described as funny, sharp, and bright—engaging the whole audience the entire way through.

To learn more about how you can hire Jenn, please visit www.jenntgrace.com/speaking.

Other Titles by the Author

Beyond The Rainbow: Personal Stories and Practical Strategies to Help your Business & Workplace Connect with the LGBTQ Market

Therapy Notes for Families: Staying organized with your child's needs

You can find all of Jenn's books at www.JennOnAmazon.com.

Listen to the *Invisible Stories* podcast

INVISIBLE **STORIES**
WRITE TO BE SEEN

Have you always wanted to write a memoir or a book about your business but never started—or never finished that draft you set aside? If you're a business owner, speaker, or entrepreneur burning to tell your story, this podcast is for you. Writing a book can be a slow, painful process. It can even open old wounds and unearth memories that are difficult to share.

In this podcast, you'll hear inspiring interviews with published authors who are striving to make a difference in the world. You'll learn how they overcame self-doubt and past hurts to speak their truth ... and how their book opened the doors to a wider audience, making a bigger impact than they ever thought was possible.

The world deserves to hear your story—and you deserve the chance to tell it.

I urge you to share your story with me. Email me at jgrace@publishyour purposepress.com and maybe we'll include your story on our website. By sharing your story with the world, you can feel a sense of relief while helping others.

Book Extras

I've created a private page on my website for you, which you can visit by going to www.jenntgrace.com/hof. You'll find reading materials, mental health resources, and even my TEDx-style talk I did about my experiences 18 months before I thought I would publish this book.

Book Club Questions

To make it easier for your book club to discuss *House on Fire*, we recommend using these questions.

1. What was your reaction to this memoir? How did it make you feel when you were reading it? What were the lasting impressions about the book or things you found yourself thinking about even days later?
2. What were some of the central themes you picked up on while reading this work?
3. What passage or quote stood out to you the most?
4. What did you think of the narrative style? Did you feel you were given the whole, true story? Or is there room for interpretation?
5. This book deals with many difficult topics: mental health, sexual assault, abuse, alcoholism. Did this book change your perspective about any of these topics or alter your viewpoint?
6. Often when people think of family, they think of blood relations. Jenn demonstrates the importance of building yourself a family unit made up of those who have the most positive influence on your life. Contrast some of the people in Jenn's adoptive family or blood relatives with those people in her chosen family. What are some of the characteristics of the positive relationships in this book?

7. There are multiple examples of a "house on fire" in this book. Discuss the significance of the title of this book and how it relates to the circumstances of Jenn's life. Why do you think the author chose to use this title?

8. Jenn used her love of the outdoors, athletic training, and running as coping mechanisms for many of the negative things happening in her life. What are some examples from your own life of how you cope with difficult situations and what are some healthy approaches to addressing negativity in your life?

9. Motherhood is a recurring theme in this book. Compare and contrast the mother figures in this book and how they may have influenced the choices Jenn made in her own life.

10. In deciding to relinquish her daughter, Jenn had to make a very difficult decision to ensure her own survival and the safety of her son. Can you think of a situation in your own life where you had to make a difficult or painful decision in the best interest of those you care about?

About PYP

Our mission at *Publish Your Purpose Press (PYP)* is to discover and publish authors who are striving to make a difference in the world. We give marginalized voices power and a stage to share their stories, speak their truth, and impact their communities. Our purpose and mission is to elevate and amplify the voices of others.

At PYP, we are fully invested in, and committed to, the success of our authors. We are focused on building long-term author relationships, not just business transactions.

We understand that publishing a book can be difficult. We go to great lengths to not only ensure your book is on track and meeting its deadline, but we also do our very best to manage your emotional overwhelm. Our work will enable you to maintain a clear focus on your vision. We act as your compass to ensure you get to your end goal.

You can follow us on social media at—

YouTube: www.PublishYourPurposePress.com/YouTube
Twitter: www.Twitter.com/PublishPurpose
Facebook: www.Facebook.com/PublishYourPurposePress
Instagram: www.Instagram.com/PublishYourPurposePress

To learn more about Publish Your Purpose Press visit www.PublishYourPurposePress.com.